STAFF BURNOUT

Sage Studies in Community Mental Health 2

SAGE STUDIES IN COMMUNITY MENTAL HEALTH

Series Editor: **Richard H. Price**
Community Psychology Program,
University of Michigan

SAGE STUDIES IN COMMUNITY MENTAL HEALTH is a book series consisting of both single-authored and co-authored monographs and concisely edited collections of original articles which deal with issues and themes of current concern in the community mental health and related fields. Drawing from research in a variety of disciplines, the series seeks to link the work of the scholar and practitioner in this field, as well as advance the state of current knowledge in community mental health.

Volumes in this series:

1. Gary VandenBos (Editor): *PSYCHOTHERAPY: Practice, Research, Policy*
2. Cary Cherniss: *STAFF BURNOUT: Job Stress in the Human Services*

Additional Volumes in Preparation

STAFF BURNOUT
Job Stress in the Human Services

CARY CHERNISS

Sage Studies in Community Mental Health 2

 SAGE PUBLICATIONS   Beverly Hills   London

For information address:

SAGE Publications, Inc.
275 South Beverly Drive
Beverly Hills, California 90212

SAGE Publications Ltd.
28 Banner Street
London EC1Y 8QE, England

Printed in the United States of America

Library of Congress Cataloging in Publication Data

Cherniss, Cary.
   Staff burnout.

   (Sage studies in community mental health; v. 2)
   Bibliography: p.
   1. Burn out (Psychology) 2. Mental health personnel. 3. Social workers. I. Title. II. Series.
BF481.C46   361.3'023   80-19408
ISBN 0-8039-1338-9
ISBN 0-8039-1339-7 (pbk.)

FIRST PRINTING

CONTENTS

For My Parents,
With Love and Appreciation

SERIES EDITOR'S PREFACE

Richard H. Price

The term "burnout" is an evocative but imprecise metaphor. It conveys the idea of energy extinguished, the fire of enthusiasm dampened. Because it is a vivid metaphor and because it conveys something real about the experience of many mental health workers, the term has become a familiar part of the professional vocabulary. The term burnout and the complex phenomenon it stands for has intrigued researchers who are trying to understand how the fledgling mental health worker's enthusiasm, hope, and desire to help can be transformed into lethargy, cynicism, and even despair in a few short months or years.

In this second monograph in the Sage Studies in Community Mental Health, Cary Cherniss shows us how the perceptiveness of a humane scientist can bring understanding and clarity to the problem of staff burnout in community mental health.

Cherniss accomplishes this task in a number of ways. First; he helps us to recognize that to understand the problem we must go beyond exploration of the individual characteristics of either the mental health worker or the client. Organizational factors, job design, social support by one's colleagues, and the role expectations communicated in the course of professional training all play a part. Cherniss broadens our vision of the meaning of the term "burnout" and places it in the context of already existing social science knowledge.

Cherniss also reminds us that not just the mental health of the client is at stake in the delivery of community mental health services, but also the mental health of the staff. The sense of purpose and meaning that is part of the helping role must be nurtured, since it is a crucial ingredient in the psychological well-being of the helper and affects the quality of care provided as well.

This book speaks to many different audiences in the field of mental health. It is a book for the new mental health worker because it can provide a framework for understanding the sometimes stressful transition from student to professional. It is a book for the staff supervisor who can provide crucial support and guidance to professionals who must give so much of themselves to others. It is a book for administrators and policy makers whose decisions about job design, client-staff ratios, and resource allocation can have a dramatic impact on the mental health worker and the quality of care they provide.

Finally, this is a book for educators in the mental health field who must be able to convey to their students both the realities and challenges of the helping role. That, and the idea that professionals can shape the circumstances under which mental care is delivered to maintain the dignity and hope of both caregiver and recipient, is a central message of this book.

AUTHOR'S PREFACE

Since I began this book just one year ago, interest in occupational burnout among human services workers has grown. In fact, many now consider burnout a "fad." Given the rapid rise in its popularity and the many superficial articles on the topic that have appeared in the popular press, this judgment is understandable. For better or worse, burnout *has* become faddish. However, it would be unfortunate if those interested in improving the human services dismissed the subject simply because it has become so popularized. For burnout in the human services does exist. It is a common reaction to job stress, and it reduces the motivation and effectiveness of many human service providers. Burnout also is a complex, social psychological phenomenon that deserves more serious study than most writers have given it. One aim of this book is to promote a more penetrating approach to the topic.

Before 1974, the term burnout had not appeared in print, and in a few years it may no longer be used. However, the phenomenon clearly existed before the term was coined, and the phenomenon will still exist when the current popularity of "burnout" passes. It is hoped that one lasting effect of this popularity will be growing and sustained interest in the broader area of personnel management in the human services. One of the unique characteristics of the human services is that workers are also "tools." It is through contact with the helper that a client changes and grows. The motivation and skill of the helper thus is extremely important, and effective management of this resource is a critical need. Unfortunately, systematic research and practice relating to personnel management have been rare in the human services. It is ironic that those who are so concerned about the human potential and welfare of others have been so careless about their own. But perhaps the "discovery" of burnout will lead to greater interest in and credibility for programs designed to promote positive career development, staff morale, job enrichment, and positive motivation.

Because job stress and burnout are part of a more general concern with human resource development, this book is intended for a diverse audience. To be sure, the book should be of interest to all those associated with the human services who are concerned about job stress and burnout in their own work and in their students, colleagues, and subordinates. However, this book also is directed at that growing group of administrators, researchers, university faculty, consultants, and trainers who are interested in personnel management in the human services.

Many people helped me write this book. Most important was Professor Richard Price, my friend and colleague in the Community Psychology Program at the University of Michigan. He first thought of the book and encouraged me to write it. Professor Seymour Sarason of Yale University, as my teacher and mentor, first stimulated my interest in this topic long before it was fashionable. Several students also have contributed to my thinking and research on burnout, including Sally Harvey, Dr. Beth Shinn, Ed Egnatios, Dr. Sally Wacker, and Anita Underwood. Barbara Toler, as always, did a splendid job of typing the manuscript and taking care of all the loose ends in my professional life. With Barb as my secretary, much of the stress that could have led to my burning out was prevented. I also want to thank Deborah and Joshua Cherniss, whose presence in my life enormously supports and sustains all of my labors.

Ann Arbor, Michigan   *Cary Cherniss*

Chapter 1

WHAT IS BURNOUT?

The problem of burnout has captured the interest and imagination of those involved in the human services. Few topics during the last five years have generated so much animated discussion among practitioners. The term "burnout" seems to have crystallized a set of attitudes and feelings about work that many have rarely discussed publicly until now. The many speeches, symposia, workshops, and published papers on the topic that have appeared, as well as the few available research studies, suggest that staff burnout is indeed a major problem and concern in the human services.

Consider the following list of incidents as an indication of the great interest in the topic that now exists:

(1) In 1976, Professor Seymour Sarason of Yale University was invited to present the keynote address at the annual meeting of the National Association of Community Mental Health Centers. He talked about the problem of low staff morale and job satisfaction. For the next two days, convention participants constantly referred to his address.

(2) Also in 1976, a symposium on burnout in the human services was presented at the annual convention of the American Psychological Association. Although the symposium was held in a room that could seat over 500 people, attendance was so heavy that many had to stand at the rear of the hall in order to listen to the presentations.

(3) An undergraduate student in one of my classes interviewed several staff and administrators in local community mental health agencies as part of a term project on burnout. Several were extremely interested in her study, and one invited her to talk about the problem at a conference for crisis center workers scheduled to be held in Chicago in just a few weeks. Although she was not a professional or noted authority in the field and the conference program had been finalized weeks before, the planning committee set aside time for her presentation. Shortly after she gave her talk, she began to receive calls from programs all over the region asking if she would do workshops or present talks on burnout to their staffs.

(4) I had a similar experience recently when I was invited to give a keynote address on the topic of professional burnout at a regional conference of the National Association of Social Workers. Following my talk, several members of the audience came up and asked if I consulted with agencies in which burnout was a problem. I am now asked to give addresses or do workshops on the topic several times each month.

(5) The lead article in a recent staff newsletter of the Michigan Department of Social Services was devoted to the topic of staff burnout.

(6) Private consulting firms have begun to offer workshops and "retreats" on burnout. A local organization has conducted several of these workshops and has had no difficulty in attracting registrants. I recently saw an impressive brochure advertising such a workshop in Big Sur, California.

(7) Articles on burnout have been published in national large-circulation periodicals such as *Human Behavior* and *Psychology Today.*

(8) In 1974, I conducted an extensive study on job satisfaction in community mental health centers (Cherniss & Egnatios, 1978a). The

results indicated that staff satisfaction with their work was quite low; in fact, compared with other well-educated workers, the average male community mental health staff person scored at only the twenty-third percentile in satisfaction with work. Female staff scored at the thirty-fifth percentile. Equally important was the response rate for this study; administrators could not believe that 94 percent of their staff willingly completed a long questionnaire. One staff member who participated in the study probably put his finger on the reason for this high response rate when he said, "We're asked to fill out forms all the time, but this is the first time anyone has been interested in finding out how we feel about the work we do. Maybe this study will help alleviate the burnout problem here."

I could cite still more incidents that point to the strength of current interest in staff burnout in the human services, but I think those listed above are sufficient. Staff members, administrators, policy makers, researchers, and students are now aware of and interested in this problem as they have never been before. They are eager to learn more about it. They are asking basic questions such as: "What is 'burnout'?" "What effects does it have on staff, clients, and programs?" "What are the causes of burnout?" "How can it be alleviated and prevented?"

Although there has been little direct research on burnout in the human services, a few studies can be used to inform the current discussion now going on in the field. Also, it seems clear that burnout is a reaction to a stressful work situation; thus, previous empirical and theoretical work on stress in the work place also can be used to further our understanding of this phenomenon. Finally, there is some useful material on the organizational dynamics and pressures associated with human service settings that can provide still more insights into the causes and cures of this problem.

The first and most basic question to consider is: What do we mean by the term, "burnout"? The current popularity of the concept is a major barrier to defining it, for it has become an appealing label for many different phenomena. It has come to mean different things to different people. Until this confusion over definitions is dispelled, little progress can be made in identifying causes and cures. Thus, our first task is to consider the various definitions that have been proposed and use them to clarify precisely what burnout is and what it is not.

SOME EXAMPLES OF BURNOUT IN HUMAN SERVICES WORK

The best way to define the concept of burnout is to describe some examples. After considering these examples, we shall be ready to define the concept in a more formal way.

Example 1. In a summer camp for emotionally disturbed children, the counselors began the summer with great energy, enthusiasm, and concern for the campers. They were selfless, idealistic, and dedicated. There was nothing they wouldn't do for their kids. But by the end of the summer, they felt exhausted and strained. They avoided contact with the children as much as possible. When they did make contact, it was usually to break up a fight or to move the kids from one activity to another. They were now short-tempered and irritable with the campers. There had been some physical abuse, even though it was strictly forbidden. The counselors sometimes made derogatory remarks among themselves about certain children and joked about their campers' quirks and failings. Many of the counselors had come to feel that emotionally disturbed children are beyond hope, too "messed up" to ever change or get better. There was much conflict among the counseling staff as well; the only thing they seemed to agree on was that the camp director was an "incompetent, devious, authoritarian bastard."

Example 2. Mary Smith was a social worker employed in a community mental health center. It was her first job since receiving her MSW. Like most new social workers, she began with great expectations. She was idealistic, committed, and hopeful. After eight months on the job, she became discouraged and demoralized about the lack of motivation and change in so many of her clients. She wanted to do family therapy, but she could never get a whole family to come in together for treatment. She was expected to spend part of her time doing consultation and education in the community. But she was not even sure what that work entailed, and certainly did not feel competent when she tried to do it. And she didn't like feeling incompetent. Going to work became more and more unpleasant. She began getting colds and flus frequently. She was less empathic and responsive in sessions with clients, except in one or two cases that were more interesting and successful than the others. She had expected that being a therapist and counselor in a mental health agency would be as fascinating as it seemed in the books she had read in college. But she became bored during many sessions with clients. She eventually quit and went back to graduate school to work on a Ph. D. in psychology.

Example 3. In its early days, this group home for youth was an exciting, innovative program. The staff was one big, happy family. No one cared about the extra hours worked. There was tremendous dedication to the youths who were thought to have great potential to change and grow. However, over time, the staff became frustrated. They were irritated by what they considered insensitive and inept administrators who were never around but made all the important decisions and were paid twice as much as the rest for working half as hard. The frequent delays in receiving pay checks and the red tape they had to go through whenever staff wanted to do something for a resident seemed to be further indication of the lack of administrative support. There also was increasing jealousy and rivalry among the staff. Cliques and conflicts emerged: afternoon versus morning staff; professionals versus paraprofessionals; black versus white. Motivation and commitment to the organization declined. Absenteeism and turnover increased. Staff rarely worked past their regular shift and became angry if they had to stay a few minutes longer because someone on the next shift was late. They began asking at staff meetings how much physical force was permitted in dealing with disruptive behavior. They also began asking why tranquilizers were not used more to help control the youths' behavior. Outside work, many members drank heavily when they came home. Many of them were having marital problems.

There are many other examples of burnout that I could present. In fact, I suspect that all of us who work in the human services have experienced at least a mild level of burnout from time to time. It bothers us. I think that is one reason why there now is so much interest in the topic. But what do we mean when we say "burnout"?

VARIOUS DEFINITIONS OF BURNOUT

Unfortunately, the term has been used in many different ways. If one starts with the dictionary, one finds the following definition: "To fail, wear out, or become exhausted by making excessive demands on energy, strength, or resources." This term aptly describes the way many staff members in community mental health programs feel some of the time. This definition suggests that burnout is the state of emotional exhaustion related to overload. Defined in this way, burnout appears to be a disease of overcommitment.

Those who have studied and written about burnout, however, have not been content with the dictionary definition. They include in their definitions certain changes in attitude and behavior that occur in response to excessive job-related demands. Maslach (1976) defined burnout as the "loss of concern for the people with whom one is working" in response to job-related stress. For Maslach, many things can happen when job-related demands become excessive; burnout refers to one particular kind of response—the tendency to treat clients in a detached, mechanical fashion.

Others have focused on changes in motivation (for example, Cherniss, 1980a). Burnout is defined as psychological withdrawal from work in response to excessive stress or dissatisfaction. Burnout is used to refer to the situation in which what was formerly a "calling" becomes merely a job. One no longer lives to work but works only to live. In other words, the term refers to the loss of enthusiasm, excitement, and a sense of mission in one's work.

Still others have used the term as synonymous with "alienation." For instance, in one study burnout was defined as "the extent to which a worker has become separated or withdrawn from the original meaning or purpose of his work—the degree to which a worker expresses estrangement from clients, coworkers, and agency" (Berkeley Planning Associates, 1977).

When one examines the "signs" or "symptoms" of burnout that have been mentioned in the literature, the meaning of the concept expands even further. Table 1.1 lists those signs and symptoms most commonly associated with burnout. Is there some way in which these various definitions of the concept can be reconciled?

TABLE 1.1   Signs and Symptoms of Job Stress and Worker Burnout in Human Service Programs[a]

1. High resistance to going to work every day.
2. A sense of failure.
3. Anger and resentment.
4. Guilt and blame.
5. Discouragement and indifference.
6. Negativism.
7. Isolation and withdrawal.
8. Feeling tired and exhausted all day.
9. Frequent clock-watching.
10. Great fatigue after work.
11. Loss of positive feelings toward clients.
12. Postponing client contacts; resisting client phone calls and office visits.
13. Stereotyping clients.
14. Inability to concentrate on or listen to what client is saying.
15. Feeling immobilized.
16. Cynicism regarding clients; a blaming attitude.
17. Increasingly "going by the book."
18. Sleep disorders.
19. Avoiding discussion of work with colleagues.
20. Self-preoccupation.
21. More approving of behavior-control measures such as tranquilizers.
22. Frequent colds and flus.
23. Frequent headaches and gastrointestinal disturbances.
24. Rigidity in thinking and resistance to change.
25. Suspicion and paranoia.
26. Excessive use of drugs.
27. Marital and family conflict.
28. High absenteeism.

[a]Drawn from Berkeley Planning Associates (1977), Freudenberger (1974), Maslach (1976), and Schwartz and Will (1961).

BURNOUT AS A TRANSACTIONAL PROCESS

Taken together, these definitions of burnout suggest that we are dealing with a transactional process. More specifically, burnout appears to be a process consisting of three stages (see Figure 1.1). The first stage involves an imbalance between resources and demand (stress). The second stage is the immediate, short-term emotional response to this imbalance, characterized by feelings of anxiety, tension, fatigue, and exhaustion (strain).[1] The third stage consists of a number of changes in attitude and behavior, such as a tendency to

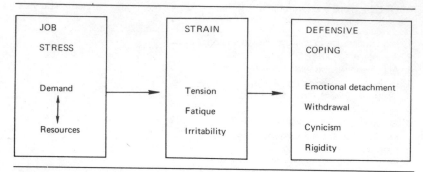

FIGURE 1.1   Transactional Definition of Burnout[a]

[a]A slightly different version of this model was suggested by Shinn (1979).

treat clients in a detached and mechanical fashion or a cynical preoccupation with gratification of one's own needs (defensive coping). Burnout thus refers to a transactional process, a process consisting of job stress, worker strain, and psychological accommodation. Specifically, burnout can now be defined as a process in which a previously committed professional disengages from his or her work in response to stress and strain experienced in the job.

This definition of burnout is appealing for at least two reasons. First, it subsumes all of the most common definitions that have been used in the literature. Second, it provides a framework for thinking about causes and solutions to the problem.

Psychologically, burnout as I have now defined it represents a response to an intolerable work situation. The process begins when the helper experiences stress and strain that cannot be alleviated through active problem-solving. The changes in attitude and behavior associated with burnout then provide a psychological escape and ensure that further stress will not be added to the strain already being experienced.

For instance, a loss of concern for the client reduces the helper's awareness of responsibility. The helper is then less vulnerable to failure that might occur in work with the client. When the helper is unable to help solve a client's problem, when the agency or related services seem to interfere with the helping process, when clients are abusive or ungrateful, the helper is less hurt if the client-helper relationship has become mechanical and distant. In other words, maintaining a detached relationship with clients serves as a defense mechanism, limiting the stress that might occur.

Maslach (1976) focused in her work on the various mechanisms used by burned-out helpers to detach themselves from clients, including the use of derogatory labels in referring to clients; impersonal, stereotyped, and superficial communication with them; going "by the book" or following a set formula; and physical withdrawal through the use of desks, offices separated from the clients by a great distance, and so on.

When the helper is experiencing a high degree of stress at work for any reason, these detachment mechanisms are likely to be used because helping relationships tend to be psychologically demanding. Empathy and caring require a considerable expenditure of psychological energy, especially when the client has many problems or is at all resistant to help. Coping with stress also depletes psychological energy. Thus, the more stress the helper experiences from any source, the less energy there is available for empathy and caring. Psychological detachment helps one conserve one's energy for the coping process, even when the client-helper relationship is not itself a major source of stress.

The loss of idealism and increasing apathy also serves a defensive function. If the helper remains committed in a situation where failure and disappointment are frequent, the strain would be great. By becoming pessimistic and cynical, the helper reduces the guilt and frustration associated with the work. Detachment from the work, like detachment from clients, helps protect the helper psychologically.

Blaming the clients or the system also serves a defensive function. As the helper begins to withdraw psychologically from the clients and from the job, as the original goals and ideals are abandoned, there can be considerable guilt. An effective way to avoid the burden of guilt is to externalize it and blame the clients or the system. This rationalizes withdrawal and preoccupation with one's own needs.

It should now be clear that burnout is a process that is self-reinforcing. Discouragement and withdrawal most likely will lead to more failure in the helping role because, as I shall discuss in the next chapter, enthusiasm, optimism, and involvement are often necessary for success. This failure leads to further discouragement, which then leads to further failure, and so on. Once the cycle begins, it is difficult to break.

To a certain extent, some detachment and realism about the limitations of the helping relationship are probably adaptive for helpers. Such an approach to one's work helps to reduce stress and, as a result, idealism and commitment persist longer. However, when detachment and "realism" become dominant, the helping relationship suffers even if the helper does not. It is impossible to know when this line is crossed.

It also should be noted that not all of the signs and symptoms listed in Table 1.1 must be present for us to say that a person is burning out. Some may be present and some not in any particular case. When we see several of these signs and changes in ourselves or others, we should consider the possibility of burnout.

In addition, burnout is not necessarily total or permanent. Job stress (that is, an imbalance between resources and demands) need not lead to severe strain. Even if it does, this strain need not lead to the defensive coping associated with burnout. Finally, even if strain produces some of those behavioral changes, the changes may be mild and temporary. For instance, even under the best of circumstances, a dedicated service provider working in an unusually supportive setting may have "bad days" when strain becomes excessive and the provider "takes it out" on clients and co-workers. In general, the greater and more chronic the stress and the more helpless the worker is to change the situation, the more likely will burnout occur and the more severe it will be.

Before considering the significance of burnout for the human services, we should end this definition of the concept by distinguishing it from related phenomena. First, burnout is not the same as temporary *fatigue* or strain, although such feelings may be an early sign of burnout. As I use the term, burnout includes change in attitudes towards one's work and clients as well as the feelings of exhaustion and tension that sometimes occur. Second, burnout is different from *socialization* or *acculturation*, the process in which a staff person's attitudes and behavior change in response to social influence exerted by colleagues or clients. For instance, McPherson (1972) described vividly how older teachers in a public school influence newer ones to emphasize order and maintain control in their classrooms. The negative changes that occur in burnout may also occur in response to the socializing influence of supervisors or co-workers. In burnout, however, these changes are a direct response to overload and stress caused by the job. Both burnout and socialization involve change in attitudes and behavior over time as a function of one's role in a system, but burnout is an adaptation to stress.

Finally, burnout should be distinguished from *turnover*. Burnout may cause staff to quit, but staff may burn out and remain on the job. (The stereotype that comes to mind is the attendant in a state institution who remains because the job pays well, is not demanding, and has great security.) Also, people may leave jobs for positive or irrelevant reasons rather than to escape a bad work situation. So while high turnover in an agency *may* be a sign of high burnout among the staff, it need not be. Burnout and turnover are different.[2]

To summarize, burnout is a process that begins with excessive and prolonged levels of job stress. This stress produces strain in the worker (feelings of tension, irritability, and fatigue). The process is completed when the workers defensively cope with the job stress by psychologically detaching themselves from the job and becoming apathetic, cynical, or rigid. As we shall see in subsequent chapters, burnout can have a significant impact on human service programs.

PLAN OF THE BOOK

In this first chapter, I have described the phenomenon of burnout and offered a transactional definition. In Chapter 2, I consider the special relevance of the phenomenon for human service programs. Specifically, there are two different aspects of the human services that are affected: First, burnout can and does occur in program staff. Thus, it represents an important problem for personnel management in those programs. However, many human service programs also have a special interest in the functioning of other community agencies such as schools, welfare agencies, correctional programs, and day care centers. Through consultation and education activities, staff members attempt to improve the effectiveness with which these other agencies deal with mental-health-related clients and issues. Staff burnout in other community agencies thus represents a legitimate and important focus for C & E efforts; for the reduction of burnout in these other settings should increase their tolerance for and effectiveness with clientele with special emotional problems and needs.

Chapter 3 provides a guiding framework for thinking about the underlying causes of organizational burnout in human service settings. Because the burnout process begins with a stressful situation, the analysis starts with a consideration of psychological stress and its causes. Basically, stress occurs when there is a perceived imbalance between resources and demands. Demands can be external (for instance, formal job requirements) or internal (for example, personal goals, needs, and moral values). One of the most important demands confronting human service staff is the demand for *competence*. The welfare and safety of their clients demand competence, and staff bring with them a strong internal desire for personal accomplishment. Thus, achieving a sense of efficacy or "psychological success" is a major driving force for the typical staff person. Any factor that frustrates this goal will contribute to stress and strain. If the staff chronically feel ineffective and helpless in their work, a psychological state referred to as "learned helplessness" will develop, and the staff will tend to use the defensive pattern of coping associated with burnout. The extent to which the staff believe they can control the factors which affect their efficacy strongly influences the degree of learned helplessness and burnout.

The next section of the book examines specific factors in the work setting, the individual, and the larger culture that influence organizational burnout in human service programs. I begin this analysis by comparing the work experiences of two human service workers. One worked in a state institution for the mentally retarded; the other worked in a small, federally funded alcoholism program. These two workers were similar in many ways, but one burned out quickly while the other became more committed, involved, and enthusiastic about the work over time. Several facets of the two work settings that seemed to contribute to the difference in experience are identified (Chapter 4).

A consideration of the work setting's contribution to job stress and burnout suggests that the "organizational design" of a program is particularly important (Chapter 5). Organizational design refers to those formal aspects of a program that can be controlled by planners and administrators. This includes the program's goals, treatment philosophies, and norms; the structure of roles and duties; and the pattern of decision-making and authority. These elements of organizational design affect the extent to which any particular role occupant experiences role ambiguity and conflict; and high ambiguity and conflict are significant sources of organizational stress and burnout. The organizational design also influences the amount of variety, meaning, learning, autonomy, and control experienced by staff. These factors also affect stress and burnout.

However, the stress that occurs in human service settings can be mitigated by supportive supervision and interaction with co-workers (Chapter 6). Supervisors and co-workers can help staff cope with stress by providing emotional support, technical help, feedback on performance, and organizational power. However, there are many factors in human service organizations that contribute to poor supervision and isolation or conflict among staff. Supervision can be adversely affected by excessive role pressures and conflicts directed at supervisors, and the supervisors may lack sensitivity or skill. Barriers to positive interaction and support among staff include differences in treatment philosophy and personal values, conflicts over differences in status or resources, and informal norms of social interaction. Thus, while supervision and interaction with co-workers can help one to cope with job stress, many barriers must be overcome first.

Burnout is almost inevitable in many kinds of work settings, but characteristics of the individual in some cases may influence the process. Personality traits, career-related goals and attitudes, previous experience, and the quality of the person's life outside of work all influence job stress and the way in which one copes with it. For instance, research suggests that those with an "external locus of control" may be more vulnerable to burnout. Also, those who are more flexible are more vulnerable to stress, but they may cope with job stress more adaptively than more rigid individuals. However, career-related goals may be even more important than personality traits; as an example, social activists who seek to effect social reform through their jobs are particularly vulnerable to stress. On the other hand, previous experience with a stressor tends to facilitate coping, especially when one has been successful in mastering it (Chapter 7).

Although organizational and individual factors are the most obvious contributors to burnout, no analysis of the phenomenon would be complete without considering the role of historical and cultural factors (Chapter 8). An especially important one is the decline of community, which has led to an increase in demand for service in public human service agencies and reduced public confidence and support for these institutions. The issue of empowerment that emerged during the 1960s led to the consumer movement, which in turn led to increased scrutiny and political pressures in the human services. The sixties also generated unrealistic expectations for change. Cultural expectations concerning professional work also have contributed to unrealistic expectations. All of these factors have generated excessive demands on service providers and/or unrealistic expectations and goals for their work.

Despite the many and complex causes of burnout in human service settings, numerous options for alleviating it are available. The work setting can be changed to reduce staff burnout, and many of the changes do not require enormous increases in personnel or resources. The strategies, which are presented in Chapter 9, fall into five general categories: staff development (including orientation, in-service training, personnel assessment and counseling, and supportive groups), the job and role structure, management development, organizational problem-solving processes, and agency goals and guiding philosophies. The optimal strategy will always depend on the specific situation. Also, every intervention designed to alleviate burnout should be carefully monitored and evaluated. However, despite the risks and obstacles, job stress and burnout can be reduced to some extent in virtually every community agency.

Thus, to summarize, burnout is a process in which a service provider psychologically disengages from the work in response to job-related stress. It is a coping strategy used when direct-action coping efforts prove futile. Burnout adversely affects clients and the organizational effectiveness of community agencies, as well as the burned-out worker. It leads to loss of concern for clients, loss of positive regard for co-workers and the agency, and emotional withdrawal from work. When a worker burns out, what was once a "calling" becomes merely a job. There are many causes, including factors in the individual, the work setting, and the larger society. In this book, we shall examine these causes and then consider concrete strategies for alleviating staff burnout in the human services.

Notes

1. Caplan et al. (1975: 3) define stress as "characteristics of the job environment which pose a threat to the individual" and strain as "any deviation from normal responses in the person."

2. This distinction between burnout and turnover was demonstrated empirically in a study of child abuse programs. The researchers found that burnout and turnover were significantly correlated, but the correlation ($r = .36$) was only a moderate one (Berkeley Planning Associates, 1977). Thus, burnout is associated with worker turnover, but it is not the same thing.

Chapter 2

THE SIGNIFICANCE OF BURNOUT
FOR THE HUMAN SERVICES

Job stress and burnout are important concerns for those involved in the human services. In fact, burnout is an important issue for at least four reasons. First, burnout clearly affects the staff member's morale and psychological well-being. Second, burnout seems to affect the quality of care and treatment provided to clients. Third, burnout may have a strong influence on administrative functioning; high rates of burnout can cause havoc in community programs. Finally, burnout in other community settings would seem to be a legitimate—in fact, necessary—concern of human service programs. Helping community caregivers to prevent job stress and burnout in their work may well be one of the most important items on the agenda of consultation and education (C & E) personnel, a way in which they can promote psychological well-being in the larger community.

THE DIRECT IMPACT OF BURNOUT
ON THE HELPING PROCESS

At this point, the research concerning burnout's effect on the helping process is of the anecdotal and case study variety; however, it is compelling, especially for anyone who has worked in a human service setting. For instance, in one of the earliest studies of burnout, Schwartz and Will (1961) carefully observed and recorded changes in staff and patient behavior on a mental hospital ward. At one point during this period, staff burnout increased sharply because of organizational changes occurring in the setting. The researchers found that as staff burnout increased, the patients were neglected and soon regressed, becoming more anxious, depressed, suicidal, and violent. When the researchers inadvertently helped to reduce staff burnout through consultation with one of the nursing staff, patient care improved and symptomatic behavior decreased.

A similar finding emerged from another early study of a mental hospital. Stotland and Kobler (1965) studied the records of a hospital covering a period of several years. They found that following every major administrative dislocation and increase in staff burnout, the patient suicide attempt rate increased. Staff burnout in this particular setting literally could be lethal for some patients.

The same trend emerged in a study of a different kind of treatment setting. Sarata and Reppucci (1974) collected various kinds of data on the functioning of a community-based prerelease program for adult offenders. Data were collected at three points in time. Between the first and second time period, the State Corrections Department ordered a special investigation of the program, a decision was made to move a drug rehabilitation program into the same physical premises, and the federal government threatened to cut off the program's funding within three months. Needless to say, tension among the staff greatly increased in response to these external threats to the program's integrity. Interestingly, the evaluation data collected shortly after these disruptions had occurred suggested a significant decline in program effectiveness. Specifically, the data showed an increase in staff ratings of client aggressiveness, an increase in client scores on the Machiavellianism scale, and an increase in the number of disciplinary actions. Also, independent observers recorded more instances of authoritarian and punitive behavior toward clients by staff during this period. In other words, organizational events that contributed to increased job stress in staff were associated with a general deterioration in measures of the rehabilitation program's effectiveness. Thus, while the available research on the topic is not as rigorous as one might prefer, there is a mounting body of evidence suggesting that job stress and staff burnout in human service programs adversely affect the helping process and the welfare of clients. These adverse effects cripple the helping process in at least two ways. First, the job stress and strain that occur in the early stages of the syndrome contribute to a state of tension, irritability, and emotional arousal that interferes with helping behavior. Second, the decline in motivation and the loss of positive feeling for clients that occur later in the process also reduce the helper's effectiveness.

Research on psychological stress (McGrath, 1970) suggests that job stress has an adverse effect on a helper's performance even before it might lead to maladaptive attitudes toward clients and work. To be sure, low levels of stress can enhance motivation and performance. However, psychological stress is more disruptive than motivating when it reaches higher levels. Furthermore, this point at which stress becomes disruptive rather than motivating varies with the complexity of the task. For more complex, ambiguous tasks, for tasks requiring thought, reflection, and creative problem-solving, relatively low levels of stress are disruptive. And if the stress persists for any period of time, the individual is likely to become demoralized and effective problem-solving is unlikely (Lazarus & Launier, 1978). Because much of the work that is done by a helper in the helping process involves complex thinking and problem-solving, we can assume that beyond very minimal levels job stress will adversely affect performance and outcomes.

A clinical social worker employed in a community mental health program described well what can happen to the helping process when job stress causes the helper to become tense, irritable, and keyed-up. This individual was interviewed as part of a study of job stress and burnout in new professionals (Cherniss, 1980a). At one point in the interview, she said:

> We really ought to start Transcendental Meditation, I guess, except I've been too busy to go to lectures. I have felt keyed-up the last few days. When I'm too keyed-up and going too fast, I start becoming ineffective with people. I become "hyper" and then I don't listen as well to my client. I'm just ready to jump in; I'm not calm enough to sit

and listen. I'm ready to talk, and I'm not listening to what's going on in them. And that, to me, is very important because when I'm calm enough, I do pick up a lot of vibes from people, unspoken things. And when I'm not picking these up, when I'm not capable of listening, then I'm not being effective, and I better slow down.

This clinical social worker was not burned out. She was involved and enthusiastic about her work and concerned about her clients. However, the role pressures associated with her job sometimes contributed to heightened stress and emotional arousal. When this arousal became too high, when she became "hyper" and "keyed-up," her behavior in therapy sessions became less effective and her clinical perception and judgment became less sensitive and accurate.

When job stress in a human service setting is chronic, the helper's motivation, involvement, and positive regard for the work and for clients may suffer; and there is some reason to believe that this increasing apathy toward, emotional detachment from, or dislike for the work also can have an adverse effect (Cherniss, 1980b). In fact, there is some research and theory suggesting that the enthusiasm, idealism, and hope of the helper are critical ingredients in counseling, teaching, and even medical care. For instance, in an extensive review of the research on classroom teaching, Lortie (1973) found evidence suggesting that the enthusiasm of the teacher is strongly associated with higher rates of student learning. In a comparative study of healing and psychotherapy in many different cultures, Frank (1973) concluded that the healer's faith and conviction in what he or she is doing is probably the most critical ingredient in the process. When the helper loses enthusiasm, when the sense of mission deteriorates, effectiveness declines. A demoralized healer does not heal, at least not as well as one who maintains zeal and commitment.

Another line of research and theory that may be relevant is the work of Truax (1966), who suggested that effectiveness in psychotherapy and counseling is strongly influenced by the degree to which the helper expresses authenticity, positive regard, and empathy toward the client. Although some critics of this work have suggested that specific knowledge and skill in clinical assessment and technique also are important determinants of effectiveness (Heller &

Monahan, 1977), this would not detract from the importance of empathy and positive regard. The most effective helpers probably combine shrewd clinical acumen with warmth and empathy toward the client. But when helpers burn out, warmth, empathy, and positive regard toward the client decline; thus, Truax's work would suggest that burned-out helpers will be less effective.

Truax's ideas have had a major impact on training in the human services. Many staff in community programs have been the recipients of programs such as "empathy training." Although these training programs may in fact contribute to increased empathy and clinical effectiveness, their impact ultimately may be limited because they do not influence the level of frustration, stress, and depression experienced as a result of factors in the current work situation. Thus, even with empathy training and good interpersonal skills, a helper's emotional responsiveness and effectiveness can be adversely affected by the negative changes in attitude that tend to occur when a helper is exposed to stress for a sustained period of time.

If job stress impinges on a helper throughout the work day, and if this stress leads to a decline in enthusiasm and empathy as the day progresses, then one would predict that clients seen at the end of the day would do less well in treatment than those seen at the beginning. Frank (1973) reported on a study of psychoanalysts and their patients that provided support for this hypothesis. Of course, one cannot be sure that the patients seen at the end of the day did poorly *because* their tired and strained analysts were less enthusiastic and empathic. The patients who choose or are assigned to these late hours initially may be poorer candidates for therapy for unknown reasons. However, the findings are consistent with the proposition that job strain contributes to lowered effectiveness in counseling and therapy.

Burnout is especially detrimental for effective and humane service delivery when it affects a large number of staff and leads to a staff subculture antagonistic to the rehabilitation goals of the institution. In Chapter 1, I noted that the final stage of the burnout process involves adoption of defensive coping strategies, such as emotional detachment and withdrawal, cynical attitudes toward clients and administration, rigidity and resistance to change, and greater preoccupation with one's own welfare and "turf." These strategies are employed by

individuals experiencing high levels of stress and strain who perceive
no direct means of alleviating the sources of the problems. However,
in some instances these coping strategies may be adopted by an entire
group within an organization. For example, the antitherapeutic, custodial norms that characterize the aid culture in many large institutions for the mentally ill and developmentally disabled (Allen et
al.,1974) originally may have developed as a collective adaptation to
job stress and organizational powerlessness. Of course, once these
norms became established as part of a subculture within the institution, new aides would be "socialized" into the value system even
before they experienced prolonged job stress and strain. Thus, high
levels of burnout within an entire group eventually may lead to the
development of an institutional climate that is antithetical to the goals
of humane care and rehabilitation.[1]

THE INDIRECT IMPACT OF BURNOUT
IN HUMAN SERVICE PROGRAMS

In addition to its direct effect on the helpers' motivation, sensitivity, and performance, burnout can affect the performance of human
service agencies in other ways as well. For instance, burnout contributes to a decline in staff job satisfaction. In one study, the correlation
between burnout and job satisfaction was −.59 (Berkeley Planning
Associates, 1977). In another, the correlation between the emotional
exhaustion scale of the Maslach Burnout Inventory (MBI) and job
satisfaction was −.35 (Maslach & Jackson, 1978). Job satisfaction, in
turn, can affect turnover, absenteeism, and interpersonal conflict.[2]
As every sensitive administrator knows, lower staff morale eventually leads to absenteeism and turnover that can disrupt program conti-
nuity and adversely affect clients because of frequent disruption and
change in their primary caregivers.

Some administrators may rationalize high staff turnover by suggesting that it ensures a steady flow of "new blood" into the program.
Especially in programs where job stress and burnout are severe, high
turnover may well be a blessing. Although there is some merit to this
argument, it ultimately rests on what may be a faulty assumption: that
the staff who leave are the ones whose performance is most adversely

affected by burnout. However, as I noted in the last chapter, a helper may burn out, developing negative patterns of thinking and action, yet remain in the job indefinitely. Staff who leave programs in which job stress and burnout are high thus may be among the most skilled and dedicated. Those who remain and who "socialize" the new staff hired into the program may be the least effective and committed to the program's goals. In other words, high turnover in human service programs does not ensure continuing high levels of enthusiasm and commitment, as some administrators have suggested. Furthermore, most administrators would agree that the costs—both financial and psychological—of constant hiring and training of new staff are high. High staff turnover can be extremely disruptive for planning and coordination in human service programs.

Thus, it is not surprising that even "hard-headed" state auditors of human service programs have become concerned about staff turnover and its social as well as economic costs. One recent state audit of a local mental health program recommended "internal program evaluation to detect reasons for high employee turnover" (Dunn, 1976). Although there are many complex economic factors influencing turnover rates, job satisfaction levels usually make a significant contribution, and burnout can greatly affect job satisfaction.

Job satisfaction also can influence service delivery in its effect on staff recruitment and hiring. For instance, the nation's mental health system today is a complex, multifaceted one in which there are many different institutional segments competing for the available professional resources. Community mental health centers must compete for staff with many other types of agencies and institutions, including universities, private clinics, state hospitals, private practice, and many non-mental-health settings which increasingly employ mental health professionals for mental-health-related components of their programs. The number of truly gifted and effective helping professionals is still limited. The best-trained and most effective mental health workers have a choice about where they will work, and usually they will gravitate to those segments of the mental health system where the working conditions are most favorable. The more talented, creative, and compassionate mental health professionals clearly want more than just a good salary; they also value stimulating, meaningful work. If community mental health jobs come to be seen as unfulfilling, the field will become an "employment slum" in the same way that the state hospitals did long ago.

Another reason for concern with burnout and job satisfaction in human services is unionization. Without a doubt, unionization of public-sector professionals has dramatically increased over the last decade (Oppenheimer, 1975). The factors which lead to unionization are numerous and complex, but certainly low job satisfaction plays a role. When unionization is a response to oppressive and frustrating working conditions, it is an understandable and sometimes effective way of improving those conditions. There surely can be little doubt that unionization frequently leads to improvements in areas such as salary and job security. However, unions often become another bureaucracy with which workers must contend (Mills, 1951). In attempting to regulate and improve working conditions through collective bargaining agreements, unions sometimes unwittingly impose even more bureaucratic control and rigidity in the work place, reducing rather than increasing the actual autonomy, freedom, and control of the individual worker. Thus, unionization which grows out of burnout and job dissatisfaction often is a mixed blessing in terms of both working conditions, broadly defined, and the quality of services received by the client.

Job stress and burnout in staff can affect human service programs in still other, more subtle, but nevertheless significant ways. For instance, Mendel (1978) suggested that job stress in these settings leads to more meetings, and more rules and regulations, increasing numbers of supervisors and administrators, greater conflict with other community groups and agencies, more staff "revolutions," increasing legalism, more authoritarian and/or bureaucratic control, and more intergroup conflict over "turf" and related issues. Also, to the extent that job stress and burnout lead to increasing isolation and withdrawal from social interaction by staff, important informal channels of communication may suffer and organizational effectiveness would be seriously impeded. Thus, job stress and burnout in staff can have numerous indirect consequences for human service programs, consequences that eventually compromise the effective and humane delivery of service.

IMPLICATIONS FOR HUMAN SERVICE PROGRAMS

Given the impact of job stress and burnout on the helping process in a human service setting, what are the most immediate implications? First, closest to home, supervisors and administrators should be concerned about burnout in their own staff. In other words, job stress and staff burnout are critical issues for personnel management in human service programs. Second, burnout that affects helpers in other community settings such as schools, churches, police departments, voluntary associations and groups, and even families may be a legitimate and important concern for consultation and education by human service staff.

Burnout and Personnel Management in Human Service Programs

Personnel management is a critical administrative concern in any human service field. Hiring, firing, and promotion decisions affect the delivery of service in clear and direct ways. Orientation and supervision of the staff are similarly critical, as are training and staff development. In all of these areas, those responsible for personnel functions also can—and do—have a significant impact on job stress and burnout. Understanding burnout and developing initiatives for preventing it thus represent a major responsibility and concern for personnel specialists in human service programs.

Although little research specifically focusing on job stress and burnout in human service programs has been published to date, there is some evidence to suggest that burnout is a problem in these settings. Cherniss and Egnatios (1978a), as part of a study on job satisfaction, asked staff in 23 community mental health (CMH) programs to complete the Job Descriptive Index (JDI). The JDI (Smith et al., 1969) consists of five scales, each measuring attitudes toward a different facet of the job. One of these scales, labeled "work," evaluates aspects of the job that seem especially important in the development of job stress and burnout. Its items include questions concerning how fascinating, routine, creative, useful, tiresome, frustrating, and endless workers perceive their jobs. The great advantage of the JDI is that it is a standard, widely used instrument with norms that allow us to compare the responses of one group of workers with those of others.

In this particular study, Cherniss and Egnatios found that the average CMH staff member placed at only the thirtieth percentile on the "work" scale. (The actual standings were the twenty-first percentile for males with at least three years of college, the thirtieth percentile for males with less than three years of college, and the thirty-fifth percentile for females.) In other words, compared with workers in other occupations, CMH staff seemed to experience higher levels of those factors that contribute to job stress and burnout. Although these findings are only suggestive, they point to the importance of job stress and burnout as personnel issues in CMH programs. Indeed, it would be difficult to argue convincingly that job stress and burnout do not occur in the CMH field. Job stress and burnout adversely affect performance, and it seems safe to assume that some job stress and burnout exist in CMH settings.[3]

Burnout and the Consultation-Education Mandate

One of the most unique aspects of community mental health is the provision of consultation and education (C & E) services. Mandated in the original federal legislation of 1963, the purpose of mental health C & E is to treat and prevent mental illness by working through "community caregivers." These caregivers include teachers, nurses, physicians, clergy, and others who represent the community's first line of defense against mental illness. Although they are not usually thought of as providers of mental health, research has suggested that individuals with emotional and interpersonal problems typically seek help from these community caregivers before turning to mental health agencies and professionals. In fact, many who experience psychological problems are reluctant to seek help from mental health resources because of the stigma attached. They feel more comfortable consulting with their family physician or clergyman (Heller & Monahan, 1977; Rappaport, 1977).

In other cases, community caregivers are thrust into the position of dealing with emotional crises and problems because of the nature of their work. For instance, a large percentage of a police officer's work involves responding to domestic conflicts. When the officers reach the scene, they are forced to take actions that may either exacerbate the conflict or contribute to a satisfactory resolution. Similarly, the way in which classroom teachers organize their classes and respond to students can have a significant impact on their students' psychological well-being. Thus, numerous kinds of community caregivers affect the community's mental health. Mental health consultation with these caregivers is intended to help them perform their roles in ways that will enhance rather than harm positive mental health.

One of the leading spokesmen in mental health consultation, Gerald Caplan (1970), identified three general types of consultation. In client-centered consultation, the primary objective is to help the consultee to deal with a particular client and problem. In consultee-centered consultation, the primary objective is to effect change in the consultee that will enable the consultee to function more effectively with all kinds of clients in the future. In program and administrative consultation, the consultant attempts to effect change in the consultee's setting that will foster positive mental health. In all three types of consultation—but especially the last two—the mental health consultant has the opportunity to improve the consultee's functioning through a focus on job stress and burnout in the consultee.

All community caregivers are vulnerable to job stress and burnout in their work. When they cannot cope with the stress in any other way, they withdraw emotionally from their work and from their clients (see Chapter 1). This lack of commitment and emotional detachment will lessen their effectiveness as agents of mental health. In fact, a burned-out teacher, police officer, or public health nurse may contribute to the interpersonal stress and difficulties of those they "serve." Thus, programs that reduce burnout in community caregivers should have a positive effect on the mental health of the community. As such, they would be examples of good primary prevention. By focusing their efforts on assessment and reduction of job stress and burnout in the consultee, mental health consultants can help to reduce the incidence of mental illness and promote positive mental health.

But what would mental health consultation with a focus on burnout look like? This is an intriguing and important question, one which opens the way for much experimentation and innovation by practitioners. However, a paper by Schwartz and Will (1961) provides a rough idea of how mental health consultation could be used to help reduce job stress and burnout in a community setting. These two authors were engaged in research in a psychiatric hospital. During the course of their studies, they worked on a ward where staff morale had deteriorated; symptoms of burnout were evident in many of the nursing staff. At one point, a new nurse was transferred to the ward, and Schwartz and Will noticed how her morale and functioning quickly deteriorated as a result of her frustrated efforts to "reach" the patients. One of the authors approached the nurse and attempted to initiate a discussion about the changes in her attitude and behavior. The nurse initially did not want to talk to the researcher about the situation; however, the researcher gently persisted, and after a week or two the nurse began talking about her frustrations and feelings. At this point, the researcher, in effect, had become a mental health consultant engaged in consultee-centered consultation focusing on the problem of job stress and burnout.

During their first few discussions, the researcher-consultant listened nonjudgmentally and encouraged the nurse to "ventilate." Gradually, he encouraged her to adopt an "attitude of inquiry" toward her own feelings, reactions, and behavior. They traced together the process of failure, stress, guilt, anger, and withdrawal through which the nurse had passed. Finally, the researcher-consultant helped the nurse formulate strategies that would help her overcome the causes and consequences of her low morale and burnout. Not only did this consultation help the nurse overcome her own burnout, but she became a "change agent" herself: through her efforts, the other nursing staff on the ward overcame their burnout. Unwittingly, Schwartz and Will discovered that mental health consultation could be used to reduce job stress and burnout in a human service setting. Presumably, the same approach could be used with other consultees working in other settings.

Another example of mental health consultation as a means of attacking job stress and burnout in the community was provided by Visher and Harris (1973). They described their experiences as mental health consultants in community job opportunity programs operated by the California State Department of Employment. In their work, they generally met with a group of employment counselors on a regular basis. The primary focus was on helping the counselors deal more effectively with problems and issues arising from their work with their clients. The clients were individuals from impoverished families whose efforts to secure employment were often hampered by emotional difficulties as well as a host of other economic, social, and political problems.

Although the employment counselors used consultation to gain more insight and skill in working with individual clients, they also began using the sessions as an opportunity to discuss their own morale problems. The authors described several examples of how mental health consultation was used to help the employment counselors cope more effectively with various types of job stress that contributed to low morale, guilt, anxiety, tension, hostility, and frustration. For instance, one staff group used the consultation sessions to discuss their feelings about communication problems in their office. Open discussion of the various issues with the consultant led to several changes in office procedures. As these changes were implemented, some of the problems disappeared and morale greatly improved.

Sometimes, simply discussing their frustrations with the consultant helped the employment counselors cope with job stresses. Although the term "burnout" was not in popular use when their paper was written, the following passage indicates that the authors confronted the problem frequently in their role as mental health consultants:

> With frequent failures, the staff members experience feelings of futility and personal inadequacy, and those who are the most sensitive feel them most strongly. They question whether they are really helping, and, they ask, "Why are we here?" Tensions and hostilities engendered by these feelings are often expressed in the form of anger at "the system," the higher-ups in the employment service, or fellow employees . . . . Consultation sessions gave staff members an opportunity to explore such feelings and to share them with colleagues and an understanding consultant, who helped them to be more objective and to comprehend the reasons behind their reactions . . . . In short, they learned to be more realistic and objective and thus more effective in their difficult and demanding jobs [Visher & Harris, 1973: 95–96].

Like Schwartz and Will (1961), these mental health professionals working in a community mental health program had never heard the term "burnout" before, nor did they anticipate that through mental health consultation they would help community caregivers cope with job stress and burnout in their work. However, their flexibility and willingness to expand their original roles in response to the community's needs and opportunities suggested another important implication of burnout for community mental health programs. If they had been more familiar with the dynamics of job stress and burnout in community human service settings, these mental health consultants probably would have been even more effective in their efforts to help consultees deal more adaptively with the problem.

In summary, burnout is a syndrome of job stress and withdrawal that seriously impedes the effectiveness of a community caregiver. For human service programs there are two important implications. First, staff burnout is a personnel problem that deserves the attention of supervisors and administrators in programs. Human service staff are by no means immune to burnout. In fact, research on the morale and working conditions of CMH staff suggests that the problem may be particularly evident in these settings. Thus, personnel managers in human service programs should focus their energies on assessment and prevention of burnout in their staffs.

The second implication is that burnout in other community caregivers working in other community settings is a logical and appealing focus for human service consultation and education. Job stress and burnout can affect any caregiver, and when this happens the community's "first line of resistance against mental illness" is weakened. Thus, consultation and education that focus on job stress and burnout in teachers, clergy, police, and informal leaders and caregivers can help promote positive mental health in the larger community.

Notes

1. An intriguing idea suggested by this line of thinking is that much of the group and organizational behavior that occurs in human service programs is essentially a strategy for coping with job stress created by the work and the way it is structured. Groups and even entire organizations may "burn out," and much of the collective behavior we observe may represent the end-point of the "burnout" process: stress-strain-defensive coping.

2. Some support for this assumption came from a recent study by Maslach and Jackson (1978). They found that mental health staff who scored higher on a self-report measure of burnout took more breaks and were more frequently absent from work (according to ratings by co-workers). Also, a recent study of 845 Social Security Administration employees found an association between burnout and an expressed interest in leaving the job within a year (Barad, 1979).

3. Specific personnel strategies for dealing with staff burnout in the human services appear in Chapter 7.

Chapter 3

THE DYNAMICS OF JOB STRESS

The first step in solving any problem is to search for its causes. Understanding the causes opens the way to solutions. In thinking about the causes of burnout in the human services, job stress is a logical starting point. In Chapter 1, I defined burnout as a transactional process that begins with job stress. Stress contributes to strain, and efforts by individuals and groups to cope with that strain lead to the emotional detachment and withdrawal commonly associated with burnout. Thus, to understand and ultimately prevent burnout, the first two questions are: (1) What, in general, causes stress? (2) What are the underlying dynamics of job stress in human service settings? Once we have answered these questions, we can identify specific factors in the individual, the work setting, and the larger society that contribute to job stress and burnout in human service programs.

THE ROOTS OF PSYCHOLOGICAL STRESS

For those who work in the human services, the concept of psychological stress should be a familiar one. Stress is a major contributor to the problems in living that bring clients to programs for help. Because human service workers should be familiar with the concept, my treatment of it will be brief.

Although there has been, and will continue to be, some debate concerning the nature of the stress response in humans, there seems to be a growing consensus regarding the general definitions and mechanisms. Both researchers and clinicians tend to define stress as a situation in which "environmental demands tax or exceed the resources of the person" (Lazarus & Launier, 1978). Whenever an individual encounters a demand, resources are mobilized to meet it. When demands and resources are relatively balanced, stress is minimal. However, when the balance is destroyed because the demands escalate or the resources for meeting them dwindle, then stress develops. This stress should mobilize the individual to take action that ultimately corrects the imbalance between demands and resources, thus reestablishing psychological equilibrium.

But what do we mean by "demand?" Again, there may be some disagreement among students of stress. In general, "A demand is such that if it is not met and neutralized somehow, there will be harmful consequences for the person" (Lazarus & Launier, 1978). Demands can be external, as when a worker faces possible loss of his or her job for failure to perform a required duty adequately, or they can be internal. Internal demands include "desired goals, values, commitments, programs, or tasks built into . . . the individual, social system, or tissue system" (Lazarus & Launier, 1978). When the individual fails to meet internal demands such as goals or values, the harm is not necessarily physical, but it is nevertheless real. Individuals generally go to great lengths to protect themselves from the damage to social or self-esteem that occurs when one of these important internal goals are not met. Thus, the harmful consequences, like the demands, can be internal and psychological.

It also should be clear that the level of stress experienced by the individual depends upon the perceived consequences of failure to meet the demand (McGrath, 1970). The more important the consequences, the greater will be the stress. When the imbalance between demand and resources threatens to produce greater harm, the stress will be greater. Thus, level of stress is a function of the perceived discrepancy between resources and demand *and* the perceived degree of harm that would occur if the demand were not met.

Although we usually think of stress and strain in connection with a situation where demand exceeds resources, when resources greatly exceed demand, psychological stress also can result (McGrath, 1970). A sense of boredom and stagnation is the common psychological response to this type of stress, and this condition of "underload" may contribute to burnout as often as does "overload." Recent work on burnout (for example, Maslach, 1976) has tended to neglect the contribution of boredom to burnout in the human services. However, research and theory concerning psychological stress, as well as the experience of many who work in the field, suggest that lack of challenge, underutilization of abilities and skills, and a paucity of intellectual stimulation are potentially important causes of burnout in mental health and related fields. Thus, in searching for causes of burnout in a work situation, one should look for factors that limit stimulation and challenge as well as those that produce overload.

Another important concept in stress theory is *coping*. When the individual (or group or organization) perceives an imbalance between demand and resources, he or she is motivated to initiate action that will remedy the situation. Coping refers to these efforts to manage demands and conflicts which tax or exceed the person's resources. Coping may be cognitive, behavioral, or a combination of the two. In other words, coping can involve active attempts to modify the person-environment relationship so that the demand is lessened or the resources increased; or coping can involve a lowering of emotional distress through modification of perceptions, attitudes, and goals. For instance, the individual may choose to minimize the harm associated with the demand by telling himself, "Oh well, it really doesn't matter that much if I can't do this." By minimizing the harm, the individual reduces the stress without actually changing the imbalance between demand and resources. Lazarus and Launier (1978) referred to this second, purely intrapsychic form of coping as "palliation."[1] Thus, coping generally takes two forms: active problem-solving and palliation.

Coping is a natural response to stress and frequently is adaptive; however, coping sometimes can have long-term consequences that are maladaptive. For instance, coping may lead to the development of destructive habits. Smoking would be an obvious example. Also, coping with stress frequently involves physiological mobilization which, if chronic, can lead to tissue damage. Peptic ulcers are a familiar example. Finally, a particular coping strategy can interfere with more adaptive behavior. The psychological defenses of avoidance or denial generally (though not always) have this effect. Thus, the stress response involves a process in which a perceived discrepancy between resources and demand that threatens to harm the organism stimulates coping behavior designed to modify the discrepancy or palliate the consequences. Ultimately, however, the outcome of the coping behavior may be more maladaptive than adaptive.

One of the most important issues in stress research and theory thus concerns the factors that influence choice of coping. Why does an individual, group, or organization choose one coping strategy rather than another in a particular instance? Lazarus and Launier (1978) suggested some tentative answers. They began by distinguishing four modes of coping: (1) search for information, (2) direct action, (3) inhibition of action, and (4) intrapsychic defense. Although natural coping behavior often involves a combination of these modes, certain kinds of situations will tend to promote reliance on certain modes and not on others.

(1) Situations characterized by high ambiguity or uncertainty will tend to favor a decrease in direct action and an increase in information-seeking. If this information-seeking fails to reduce the ambiguity, the intrapsychic mode may come to be emphasized. For instance, the individual simply may try to avoid thinking about the situation and the potentially harmful consequences.

(2) A severe degree of threat-harm usually will lead to more desperate and primitive modes of coping, such as panic, rage, and confused thinking.

(3) A situation characterized by high conflict will tend to immobilize direct action and lead instead to intrapsychic defense. An example would be a dispatcher in a plant who is urged to speed up deliveries by sales personnel at the same time that the delivery people are telling him that they cannot and will not work any faster. A person caught in such a conflict is likely to distort the messages received

from one or both sides in order to reduce the perceived conflict and stress.

(4) Helplessness also immobilizes direct action. If the individual perceives no way of dealing with the situation directly, then intrapsychic modes of coping again will tend to dominate. Thus, characteristics of the situation (as well as many other kinds of factors) will influence the choice of coping strategy.

These notions about the general dynamics of psychological stress can now be used to clarify and direct our search for the causes of burnout in human service work. First, as a type of stress response, burnout will develop as a reaction to a situation in which there is an imbalance between demand and resources. A careful analysis of a helper's work situation should identify different kinds of demands and different kinds of resources for meeting those demands. The demands may be both external and internal. For instance, a supervisor's insistance that certain paperwork which is overdue be turned in by the end of the week probably would be a purely external demand. On the other hand, a psychologist's desire to capture the "essence" of a client's functioning in a written test report would be a primarily internal demand. Either type of demand may be compelling and, if the resources (for example, time, energy, skill, or motivation) are not available and the harm of failing to meet the demand is perceived to be high, then the individual will experience considerable stress. Thus, an attempt to analyze and prevent burnout in a human service setting should be guided by the following questions: What demands, internal and external, are made on the helpers? What resources are required to meet these demands? Are the necessary resources available?

Furthermore, the way in which a helper chooses to cope with stress on the job also seems critical for the emergence of burnout. Burnout involves a particular way of coping with job-related stress, one which emphasizes withdrawal, detachment, avoidance, lowering of goals, and blaming others. These are intrapsychic modes of coping with stress. Theoretically, a helper who is experiencing stress could employ alternative modes of coping. However, the burnout syndrome involves a clear choice to use intrapsychic psychological defenses rather than active problem-solving methods. According to Lazarus

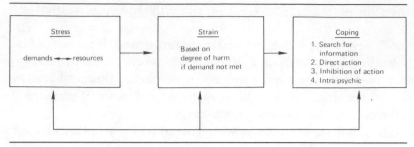

FIGURE 3.10   The Stress-Coping Cycle

and Launier (1978), situations characterized by high ambiguity, conflict, and helplessness will favor the use of withdrawal and intrapsychic defense. We shall see in this and subsequent chapters that these
conditions occur frequently in bureaucratically organized human service programs. An attempt to understand and prevent burnout thus
should consider the specific causes of uncertainty, conflict, and organizational powerlessness in any situation. Other factors in the individual and work setting that contribute to the use of psychological
detachment in response to job-related stress also should be considered. These considerations concerning the relationships among
stress, coping, and burnout are presented schematically in Figure 3.1.

EFFICACY: A PRIMARY CONCERN OF
HUMAN SERVICE WORKERS

We have seen that psychological stress and strain occur when there
is an imbalance between resources and demands. Demands can be
internal as well as external. Although there are many kinds of specific
demands directed at human service workers, a general one which
seems of great psychological significance in the development of
burnout is the demand for competent, effective performance
(Cherniss, 1980a). The typical staff member in a human service
program strives to achieve a sense of efficacy in his or her work. If
this goal is blocked, the person's self-esteem is threatened and the
stress response is strong. Thus, any factor that thwarts a worker's
efforts to perform effectively or to feel effective will be a major
source of job stress, strain, and burnout.

For all individuals, competence seems to be a primary need (White, 1959). The strength of this need may vary with the culture. Our society is particularly competitive, achievement-oriented, individualistic, and meritocratic. In such a cultural milieu, the need for competence will be especially strong; self-esteem, social status, economic security, and political power are strongly tied to competence.

Furthermore, there is reason to believe that the quest for competence and efficacy is especially critical for those engaged in human service work. For instance, in one study, staff employed in community mental health programs indicated that experiencing a sense of accomplishment in their work was the single most important contributor to their job satisfaction (Cherniss & Egnatios, 1978a). If they felt that they were effective, all other annoyances and dissatisfactions tended to seem relatively unimportant. Similarly, in a study of mental retardation programs, Sarata (1972) identified lack of client progress as the major source of dissatisfaction for staff. And in a study of public school teachers, Lortie (1975) noted that teacher satisfaction was closely tied to achieving "results with students" and feeling that one had "influenced students." Thus, empirical research suggests that achieving a sense of efficacy is perhaps the strongest job-related goal human service providers bring to their work.

A consideration of the work situation in the human services suggests why personal effectiveness, or lack of it, is such a critical factor in burnout. First, human service work involves direct responsibility for the well-being of other people. If a salesperson or factory worker makes a mistake, the consequences usually are not as grave. As Kramer (1974) noted, Ford Motor Company has recalled 500,000 automobiles because of errors in design or manufacture, and this action does not greatly disturb the public. But the "recall" of clients by a community mental health center because of errors in treatment is unthinkable. The public's reaction would not be so mild.

The responsibility for other people's lives thus represents a major factor contributing to the special importance of efficacy in human service work. As one public health nurse put it:

There are a lot of concerns about this job, thinking about all these people in the community that are kind of your responsibility. And I think about it! Like just this weekend, I had this woman who was having some problems, and I thought about her all weekend, just thinking about what I can do and what I should do. There's a little bit of pressure there, I'd say! [quoted in Cherniss, 1980a].

A high school teacher expressed the same feelings about the importance of efficacy in her work:

I really feel that I have a responsibility to be prepared for the students. I'm not just in a job. What I teach these kids is going to be important to them some day, I think—I hope. I don't feel I have a right to toy with them. They expect certain things from me as I expect certain things from them, and that gives me the get-up-and-go [quoted in Cherniss, 1980a].

In the human services, the responsibility for others' well-being makes the demand for effective performance especially strong. It is a demand that is communicated by clients, supervisors, colleagues, and, often most of all, oneself. One would expect that if helpers feel they lack the resources necessary to meet this demand, the stress and potential for burnout would be high.[2]

A second aspect of human service work that makes the demand for competence so strong is the personal significance of the work. Human service work is expected to be more than just a job. It is a *calling*. One's identity and self-esteem thus will be more tied to the outcome of one's work than would be the case in other occupations. One prepares to become a social worker, psychologist, teacher, clergyman, nurse, or physician in a way that one does not prepare to become a factory worker, bartender, or post office employee. The greater preparation is emotional as well as financial and intellectual. The human service worker, particularly the professional, invests him or herself in the work long before beginning practice. The worker's identity merges with his or her work in a way that would seem strange in another type of occupation.

This greater psychological investment is not simply associated with professionalization. For instance, one could think of a parent as a human service worker—probably our society's most important human service worker. Even though parenthood is not considered a profession, and there is no formal training required to become a parent, many parents invest heavily in their parenting role. Their self-esteem is strongly affected by how well they perform this role. Thus, whether or not the human service worker has prepared for the role through a lengthy, formal training process, this type of work often will be more closely tied to one's identity and sense of self than would be the case for many other types of work, and the demand to perform competently will be great.

Given the importance of human service work for both the helper and the helped, it is not surprising that competence and effectiveness are such important goals for the helper. The demand for competence is one that cannot easily be denied. It is competence that human service workers most admire in others and want for themselves. Although the following quote came from a public health nurse, it conveys a feeling about being effective and competent that anyone engaged in human service work probably could identify with:

> I met this consultant who I found out graduated two years before I did. She's come back as a mental health consultant for the Visiting Nurses Association. She got out of school, went to Boston for a year, then went to Ohio State to get her master's in family counseling within nursing; and this girl is just . . . you know, she doesn't wear a white uniform. She's really the only person in our agency who does this kind of work. So you go to her when you have problem patients, psychologically, that you would like help with, and this girl, I have so much admiration for her. She's unreal, what she does. To watch her work! You have a family trouble, and you go in and she sits them all down and she says, "Now look your father in the eye and tell him you love him. You love him? Tell him you love him." She solves a tremendous amount of problems. She has gone so far. I guess I look at her and I think that's the way it should be. I think when I saw her, it kind of made me fit in a lot of little pieces of things I know I would like to do, but I didn't know where to go with them. And I've really never met another nurse that I felt I could use as a role model so much [quoted in Cherniss, 1980a].

Unfortunately, there are several features of work in the human services that make effectiveness elusive. The quest for competence frequently is a frustrating and difficult one. As one mental health worker succinctly put it, "What you can do for a client and what you should do are two different things." Even when the helper is personally well suited for the work (skillful, sensitive, a "natural"), and even when the helper has received the best possible training for the work, there are several aspects of work that ultimately limit one's sense of efficacy.

One such aspect is lack of feedback from clients. Clients rarely come out and tell a human service worker how well they are doing and how much they appreciate the help. And even when they do, can one accept such feedback as evidence that one in fact has been effective?

The lack of feedback from clients thus is related to another factor: lack of data on outcomes more generally. If the client feedback is rare and of dubious validity, what other kind of feedback is available? Unfortunately, most human service work, compared with other types of work, offers little feedback of any kind. Even with the current emphasis on accountability and program evaluation in the human services, there still is little in the way of ongoing evaluation that provides frequent, relevant feedback to the practitioner. So often the helper must work in the dark, not knowing how much his or her efforts are succeeding. Consequently, the need for a sense of efficacy is thwarted.

Still another problem to be confronted is what Lortie (1975) called "authorship." Even if the helper in a human service program could acquire reliable, valid feedback on the client's psychological change and growth, to what extent are those changes a direct result of the helper's will and effort? Clients clearly do not exist in a vacuum; there are many forces impinging on them all the time. Their weekly or even daily sessions with a therapist may be of great psychological significance, but this therapy represents only one of many forces in their lives. Thus, if and when clients do improve, the helper's contribution inevitably must be in doubt, and this fact of life further limits the helper's sense of efficacy.

The extent to which clients are influenced by other forces suggests yet another impediment to efficacy: The helper's lack of control over many of those systematic forces that shape—often in personally destructive ways—the world in which clients must live. An example of one of those forces is the welfare system, an important factor in the lives of many clients served by human service programs. Anyone who has tried to help these clients will have had experience like the following one provided by a legal aid attorney:

> You get very frustrated with a case like this. A woman had five or six children living in her house. The husband had moved out and was living in the garage. He was working and not giving the wife a cent to buy food, to heat the house, or anything for the kids. But according to the Department of Social Services [welfare], *he was living on the premises, he was working, and therefore they did not qualify for welfare.* And there was nothing they would do [quoted in Cherniss, 1980a].

Even this attorney's own system became an obstruction: The family's income made them ineligible for legal aid as well. Therefore, the attorney could not help this woman get money from either welfare or her husband. Such a situation obviously is not conducive to the development of a sense of efficacy in a human service professional.

Sometimes even the clients seem to be looking for ways to make the helper less effective. Effective performance in the human services usually requires a level of active cooperation and assistance by the client that is not required in other kinds of work. An "acting out" adolescent client may resist a therapist's efforts in a way that a piece of metal or machinery never would resist a worker on an assembly line. Again, workers in human service programs probably could furnish many examples like the following one, related by a public health nurse: An elderly woman was suffering from a number of medical problems, as well as the loneliness and impoverishment that often accompany old age. This nurse had put a great deal of time and effort into the case. She had made several visits to the home, brought in a physician to examine the woman's skin problems, and arranged for a senior citizens group to become involved. However, despite all of these efforts, the woman actively resisted help and became increasingly depressed and apathetic. During her last visit to this patient, the woman told the nurse, "I don't know why you're bothering with me; I just want to die."

How did the nurse respond to this case? How *could* she respond?

As she put it:

> You know, I think about her. I can't help it. She's in this big house, her
> plumbing doesn't work, no hot water. But she's been seen by a doctor,
> and the neighbors are aware of the problem, so I guess that's all we can
> do right now. She'll probably just stay in her house and die [quoted in
> Cherniss, 1980a].

If there is any doubt that such an incident can shake a professional's
sense of competence, it should be dispelled by the comments offered
by this nurse when asked how she felt after the incident had occured:

> It was kind of like a rejection sort of thing . . . I thought, "Gee, what's
> wrong with me? What did I do? You know, I might have done some-
> thing wrong. Maybe I just turned her off. Maybe it was just a personal-
> ity conflict." But I didn't see it, and that's the thing that bothered me,
> that I didn't have enough insight to see the problem. So yeah, it
> bothered me [quoted in Cherniss, 1980a].

The demand for competence is strong in nursing, mental health,
and other human service work. If a client is uncooperative, resistant,
or even apathetic, even the most sensitive and psychologically skillful helper may not be successful. To put it in terms of the stress-strain-
burnout framework presented earlier, client motivation is a necessary
resource for meeting the *demands* of the helping relationship. Such a
gap between resources and demand will create much stress and strain
for the helper. However, over time, a helper working with many such
clients in a community setting may feel increasingly helpless to actively change these situations. When this occurs, the helper may
choose to "cut" his or her emotional "losses" by withdrawing emotionally from the work—stop trying and adopt a fatalistic attitude
toward the clients and their problems. In other words, the helper may
burn out. Thus, the lack of client motivation and cooperation, and the
other aspects of human service work I have noted, prevent the helper
from adequately responding to the demands of the job; the quest for
competence and efficacy is thwarted. The result is increased stress
and the potential for burnout.

PSYCHOLOGICAL SUCCESS: THE NEED FOR PREDICTABILITY AND CONTROL

The critical importance of achieving a sense of efficacy in one's life has been recognized by many psychological theorists. One of the first was Kurt Lewin (cited in Hall, 1976), who argued that successful performance of a valued task leads to enhanced self-esteem, a desire to set higher goals, and greater commitment and motivation. However, Lewin made a distinction between self-perceived or "psychological" success and externally defined success. *Psychological success* occurs when there is a challenging but attainable level of aspiration, the goal is defined by the person, the goal is central to the person's self-concept, and the person works independently to achieve the goal. If these conditions are not present, even a successful performance will not enhance esteem, goal-setting, and task involvement nearly as much. The success will be less meaningful. Thus, jobs that are high in autonomy, challenge, and feedback will be more likely to contribute to psychological success, and the incidence of burnout will be lower.

The relationship between Lewin's concept of psychological success and burnout was made especially clear by Argyris (1957). He asked, "What happens when a person must work in a situation structured for failure, a situation in which success occurs rarely, or the conditions for *psychological* (i.e., self-controlled) success are not present?" His answer was that the person will increasingly use intrapsychic defense. The result will be apathy, increased concern with material rewards, heavy use of psychological defense mechanisms (such as denial, avoidance, and repression), fighting the organization, changing one's position, or leaving the organization. If these coping strategies fail, the person may become more dependent and passive, his or her time perspective will shorten, self-esteem and self-confidence will decrease, and fear of new tasks will increase. The person also will increasingly *expect* to fail, give up quickly, lose interest in work, and tend to blame others.

Thus, achieving psychological success appears to be a strong internal "demand." If, as for other demands, the resources for meeting it are not available, harm to self-esteem is imminent. Stress and strain develop, and the individual uses various coping mechanisms.[3] Frequently, the factors that frustrate the quest for psychological success seem to be outside of the individual's control; thus, the individual must resort to intrapsychic coping measures, and the outcome frequently is burnout. Therefore, any factor that blocks psychological success in work is a possible contributor to burnout. Human service workers seek to achieve a sense of efficacy and psychological success through two avenues. The first is task-accomplishment: Competently and successfully performing a task that contributes to the goal of enhanced well-being for clients clearly will enhance psychological success. The second involves the ability to control the work environment. Organizational obstacles to effective task performance inevitably will occur in human service programs; however, if the worker is able to predict and control these obstacles, psychological success will not be threatened and may even be enhanced.

Psychological success requires the ability to predict and control one's environment. Lack of control and an inability to predict important events have been shown to produce considerable psychological stress and disturbance in humans (Seligman, 1975). Unfortunately, those who work in publicly supported, bureaucratically organized human service programs frequently experience a sense of powerlessness in their jobs, an inability to control or even predict important forces that influence their work. Consequently, psychological success is thwarted. (More material on this facet of human service work will be presented in Chapter 4.)

The positive psychological effects of control and predictability were demonstrated by the following study (Seligman, 1975). Individuals were placed in situations where they would have to take electric shock. In one group, the subjects could not control when the shock would occur, nor did they know in advance when it would occur. In a second group, the subjects could not control the onset of shock, but they were given a warning just before the shock occurred so that it was predictable. The last group could control the onset of shock. The results showed that stress and strain were greatest when subjects lacked both control and predictability. Predictability lessened the strain associated with the shock, and control lessened it still more.

Even when the outcomes are positive, lack of control over those outcomes can have detrimental effects. According to Seligman (1975), individuals who receive positive reinforcement independent of their responses manifest the same motivational and emotional disturbances that occur when they are unable to control traumatic events. Helplessness thus contributes to stress and strain independent of any other occurrences. Even when the outcomes are benign or positive, helplessness is destructive. Thus, helpers in an unpredictable human service setting who lack control over their work environment will experience stress and may burn out.

THE ROLE OF LEARNED HELPLESSNESS IN BURNOUT

Thus far I have suggested that a central goal for human service workers is to achieve psychological success in their work. Control and predictability in the work setting are necessary in order to achieve this goal. Any factor that contributes to helplessness, unpredictability, and/or failure will produce considerable stress that may result in burnout. However, I also noted that those who experience stress and strain can use a variety of different coping strategies, only some of which will lead to burnout. What leads a human service worker to use the defensive coping strategies associated with the burnout phenomenon?

One possible cause of the defensive coping associated with burnout is "learned helplessness." Seligman (1975) defined helplessness as a situation in which the outcome occurs independently of all voluntary responses by the individual. In other words, when no action by the individual has any effect on what occurs, the individual is helpless. *Learned* helplessness is the *belief* that one has no control over important rewards and punishments. This belief has developed as the result of previous experiences of helplessness.

In the original research on learned helplessness (Seligman, 1975), dogs were placed in boxes with electrified floors and a barrier separating the two halves. For one group of animals, it was possible to escape the shock by jumping over the barrier. For the other group, no escape was possible. This second group, in other words, was helpless. The researchers found that after several training trials the two groups responded differently to the onset of shock. The group that had had "escape training" would struggle actively to escape when placed in a box and shocked. However, the group that had experienced helplessness made no effort to escape. Instead, they merely cowered in a corner of the box and whimpered pathetically. Their helplessness had become *learned*. Even when the barrier was removed so that the animals could easily escape from the shock, the learned helplessness group remained in the electrified half of the box, passively receiving extremely high levels of electric shock. These animals literally had to be dragged from one side of the box to the other numerous times before their learned helplessness was extinguished and they once more tried to escape on their own when given shock in the training box.

According to Seligman (1975), learned helplessness has three deleterious effects on an organism. First, motivation is impaired: The desire to initiate action, to solve problems, and to overcome obstacles declines sharply. Second, the ability to believe that a response has worked is impeded; in other words, a person who has frequently experienced helplessness in a situation will miss or deny information suggesting that control now is possible. Third, lack of control disturbs one's emotional balance, causing depression, anger, and anxiety.

Thus, when prolonged helplessness leads to *learned* helplessness, an individual's coping behavior will be affected. Specifically, those who believe that they can control a situation will tend to perceive the environment more accurately and will be less likely to resort to the intrapsychic defenses associated with burnout. Some evidence for this comes from a study by Dweck (1972), who found that when children were trained in a problem-solving situation to believe that their failures were due to their own lack of effort and not factors beyond their control, they were less likely to fall apart and use primitive psychological defenses when they subsequently experienced frustration and failure. Learned helplessness thus may be the ultimate source of burnout in human service workers.

However, we shall see in the following chapters that learned helplessness, psychological failure, and burnout need not be inevitable in human service settings. Differences in attitude, skill, the structure of

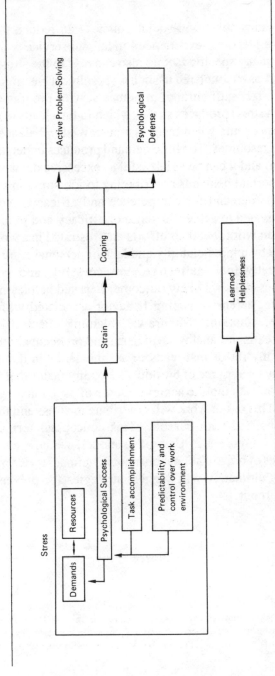

FIGURE 3.2 Basic Sources of Burnout in Human Service Programs

jobs and organizations, and social policies can reduce the failure, stress, and helplessness experienced in human service work. By the same token, many specific factors also can *add* to the stress, failure, and helplessness encountered in such work, almost ensuring burnout.

To summarize, staff burnout in human service programs is a process in which stress produces strain, which in turn leads to defensive coping. Stress occurs when there is a perceived imbalance between demands and resources. Too little demand produces understimulation and boredom, and it can be as stressful as excessive demand. One of the most important demands contributing to job stress in the human services is the demand for competence and efficacy. Workers are strongly motivated to achieve a sense of efficacy and psychological success in their work, but their efforts are frustrated in a work setting characterized by unpredictability and lack of personal control. When staff chronically feel ineffective, unsuccessful, and powerless, learned helplessness is a likely outcome. Learned helplessness leads to the passive, defensive coping behavior associated with burnout (for example, emotional withdrawal, blaming clients for lack of progress in treatment, apathy, cynicism, and preoccupation with the self). Thus, any factor that leads to an imbalance in demands and resources may be a source of burnout. Also, any factor that frustrates the staff person's attempts to achieve a sense of psychological success and control in his or her work will contribute to stress and the coping behavior associated with burnout. This conceptual formulation is summarized in Figure 3.2. Using this model, we now can identify specific causes of organizational burnout in human service programs. This analysis ultimately will suggest strategies for preventing and alleviating burnout.

Notes

1. The similarities between "palliation" and the psychoanalytic concept of "defense" are obvious (Freud, 1936). Although psychoanalytic thinkers have tended to view intrapsychic defenses such as avoidance, denial, and repression as primarily maladaptive and destructive, recent stress theorists such as Lazarus (1966) and Mechanic (1962) have taken a more neutral

position. They suggest that palliation may be highly adaptive in some situations; in fact, it sometimes may be more adaptive than problem-solving.

2. Research has suggested that people with close personal responsibility for the lives of others are more often victims of stress-related disease such as peptic ulcers, myocardial infarction, hypertension, and diabetes (Cobb, 1973).

3. Recent thinking on the concept of "flow" suggests a similar process. According to Csikszentmihalyi (cited in deCharms & Muir, 1978), the experience of flow occurs when task difficulty slightly exceeds competence. Large discrepancies lead to boredom or anxiety. Flow deprivation is associated with feeling more tired and less relaxed, creative, reasonable, and spontaneous.

Chapter 4

SOURCES OF BURNOUT
Two Case Studies

In searching for sources of burnout in a human service setting, there is a tendency to focus on a single level of analysis. For some, that level is the individual; they ask, "What kind of person is most likely to burn out?" For others, the investigation focuses on the organizational level. Here, the central question becomes, "In what kind of job, in what kind of organization, is burnout most prevalent?" Or, to put the question in a slightly different form, "What are the characteristics of jobs and organizations that contribute to or prevent burnout?" Finally, there are a few who emphasize the societal or cultural level of analysis. Their central question always is, "What aspects of our society contribute to burnout in human service occupations?"

Obviously, one can find sources of burnout at each of these three levels: societal, organizational, and individual. In fact, an adequate treatment of the problem must address each of these levels and recognize their interrelationships.

There are two reasons for beginning with the organizational level. First, differences in jobs and organizations probably are more powerful sources of burnout than are differences in individuals. Some support for this proposition comes from a study of burnout in child abuse programs, a study which assessed the relative contribution to burnout of various factors (Berkeley Planning Associates, 1977). The researchers found that "organizational climate variables" such as leadership behavior, communication, and clarity of goals were more significant than individual demographic variables such as sex and educational level. Of course, one study does not prove the proposition. However, any human service professional who has worked in both a large, custodial, bureaucratically enmeshed state mental hospital and a small, relatively autonomous, progressive clinic serving a primarily young, attractive, verbal, and well-educated client population will probably appreciate the enormous difference that organizational factors can make. Although I know of no research on the subject, it seems safe to predict that organizational burnout in the large state hospital would be higher than in the small, progressive clinic. There are many settings in the human services that seem to be structured for burnout.

However, there is a second reason for focusing first on the job and organization: It is ultimately easier to reduce the incidence and severity of burnout by intervening at this level. This statement might seem odd to those who have been frustrated in their attempts to change a human service organization. However, changing individuals is not easy, either. One clearly confronts the same problems of internal resistance and lack of control over critical contingencies when attempting to change either individuals or settings. And those who have tried to find and hire the "right kind" of individual for a human service job will recognize that our knowledge and ability to make an impact at this point also will be limited.

Individual behavior is strongly influenced by the social setting. We usually can change a person's attitudes and feelings more easily by changing the structure of his or her roles than by working directly with the person. Of course, we must first gain the power to change or create the organization's role structure. However, once we are able to do this, we are in a much better position to reduce the incidence of burnout. For instance, it is easier to reduce "role conflict" (an organizational-level source of burnout) than to change an adult's "locus of control" from external to internal (an individual-level source of burnout). Furthermore, for the amount of time and skill necessary to modify one person's locus of control, one could reduce role conflict for a large number of people. In other words, interventions at the organizational level not only tend to be more effective, but they also have the potential for affecting more individuals for the same resources.

Many of the factors in a work setting that contribute to job stress and burnout are revealed by comparing and contrasting actual experiences. In fact, much can be learned by studying the work situations of mental health professionals who differ in their degree of burnout. A particularly good comparison is provided by two social workers who participated in a study of burnout in new professionals (Cherniss, 1980a).These two individuals were similar in numerous respects; however, one became burned out after only nine months in her job while the other became increasingly involved, committed, and enthusiastic about her work during that period.

Both of these individuals had received masters' degrees in social work within the last year. Both were women in their mid-thirties who had been married but were now divorced. Both worked with client populations that traditionally have been less successful candidates for treatment in the human services (the mentally retarded and alcoholics). Both began their jobs with great anticipation and a sense of purpose. Despite these similarities, only one showed signs of burnout during the first year of work.

A STRESSFUL WORK SETTING

The person who burned out, whom I shall call Karen Mikelson, worked in a large state institution for the retarded. Most of her time, however, was spent in a distant county where she supervised the community placements of retarded clients who had been discharged from the institution. The remaining time she worked at the institution where she was responsible for a number of clients who were still institutionalized.

The first important source of stress in Karen's job was the clientele. She had worked with the retarded before, but these previous experiences involved an "educable" population. In her current job, she

worked with a "lower functioning" group, people who were expected
to learn very little, people who were dependent and could not even
take care of their physical needs. For these clients, the goal was
simply to ensure that their physical needs were being met. The emphasis was on maintenance, not rehabilitation. Although Karen did
not complain specifically about this aspect of her job, she was deprived of an important source of gratification, meaning, and stimulation in work: There were apparently few opportunities for experiencing a sense of efficacy or utilizing the skills she had developed during
her training.

Matters were made even worse by the case load. Karen was responsible for the supervision of over 90 clients spread over a two-
county area, as well as 50 inpatients still awaiting discharge from the
institution. She said that she was frustrated because all of her time
was consumed by crises that needed immediate attention (such as a
client who suddenly needed a new placement within 48 hours). The
heavy case load prevented her from helping home operators improve
their management practices. The reactive crisis orientation allowed
little time to work with individual clients or help develop new community resources. Thus, the size of her case load, as well as the type
of client with whom she worked, prevented Karen from feeling she
was efficient; she often felt as though she were just "treading water."

Another major source of stress for Karen was organizational conflict and lack of support within the institution. Karen was one of six
social workers employed by this institution. Together, they constitut-
ed the social services department. In this medically oriented setting,
the social services department was one of the smallest and most
marginal. According to Karen, the department was really not "accepted" within the institution. The work they did was neither valued
nor understood by other staff. In fact, Karen believed that many staff
thought the social workers were merely "transportation aides." At
one point she summed up this source of stress in her work: "You just
don't get support for breaking your neck out in the community."

Relations among the various departments were strained. Competition, jealousy, and rivalry characterized their interactions. Karen said
that the one thing social workers had in common was their defense
against a "common enemy." Cooperation and collaboration between

different staff groups was actually discouraged. For instance, a proposed orientation group for new residents was vetoed by the department heads involved because the group was to be co-led by a nursing aide and a social worker. Such collaboration was regarded as "unwise."

Thus, the intergroup conflict within the institution and the social service department's marginal and precarious position gave rise to an emphasis on caution and a distaste for innovation and creativity. There developed a rigid, restrictive set of norms designed to ensure that staff would not further weaken the department's position in the institution. According to Karen, her director's attitude was, "Don't rock the boat. Don't confront the issues here. Don't make waves."

Although this attitude may have been an appropriate one given the department's marginal position within the institution, Karen found it intolerable. She said that she was just "not like that at all." Her style was to confront problems, not cover them up. Initially, Karen attempted to change the restrictive, bureaucratic climate of her department. She spoke up at staff meetings. She challenged policies that seemed to serve trivial bureaucratic purposes at the expense of clients. Unfortunately, Karen's co-workers were unwilling to support her attempts to change things. She was labeled the "pushy, aggressive, malcontent" in the group. Once this occurred, people just "tuned out" whenever she said anything critical. They stopped listening to what she said, and she lost what little influence she might have had. Consequently, her frustration increased still further. She came to believe that she could have no impact on the system, that it was hopeless. She coped by withdrawing. She avoided the institution and spent as much time in the community as possible.

However, even in the community, Karen was still a state employee, and decisions made at the state level further contributed to her sense of frustration and powerlessness. She said that the state's priorities concerning after-care planning kept changing without notice or reason. After this happened a few times, she could not become enthusiastic about, or strongly committed to, any particular programmatic thrust; for there was always the sense that it would only be temporary.

Karen also received little help or support for her efforts to cope with this confusing and demanding work situation. When she started her job, she received no formal orientation to the complex environment in which she would be working. She was told simply to spend the first week reading through a set of rules and procedures that were meaningless to her at that point. True to form, there *was* a formal, two-week orientation program—five months after she had begun her job! (In the interests of bureaucratic efficiency, the orientation program was delayed until there was an "adequate" number of new employees to participate in it.) Needless to say, this orientation program was not very useful by the time Karen participated in it.

Another potential source of support—supervision—became another source of conflict and strain. Initially, Karen had two supervisors: the director of social work and the supervising social worker. These two individuals differed in their views, frequently argued with one another, and avoided interaction with each other whenever possible to avoid further conflict. Consequently, they often gave Karen conflicting messages. Fortunately, the director resigned six months after Karen began the job, eliminating this source of conflict. However, until the decision concerning his replacement was finally made, this uncertainty was yet another source of tension for Karen and her co-workers.

Even when the supervision issue was resolved and Karen only had one primary supervisor, she continued to receive conflicting messages. On the one hand, her supervisor seemed to tell her, "Go out and do the job, you're competent. I trust you." But then Karen would come back a few days later, and her supervisor would say, "What's going on? What are you doing out there? I want to know everything that you do before you do it."

Karen usually received no supervision at all. Much of the time her supervisor was not available for consultation. Supervision meetings would be scheduled and then canceled at the last moment. When Karen and her supervisor did meet, her supervisor simply provided her with administrative information. Her supervisor seemed to be uninterested in and/or unable of giving Karen the kind of ongoing emotional support and technical assistance that could increase her effectiveness in her work. Again, the primary concern in supervision seemed to be that Karen do nothing that might "rock the boat."

Karen also did not receive much support from her peers. She said that there was little "informal sharing" among the social work staff. Because they supervised placements in different counties, they only came together as a group when staff meetings were scheduled. Days could go by without their paths crossing. When they did come together for staff meetings, the structure of those meetings prevented them from engaging in a genuine exchange of ideas and discussion of professional issues. The director set the tone for the meetings; the tone was formal, businesslike, and bureaucratic. The director used the meetings to communicate information concerning administrative rules, changes in policies, and so on. The director controlled the content and flow of the meeting. The message that Karen and the others received was that this was the "director's meeting," and the director wanted to use the meeting only to tell staff what they should be doing. Emotional support, mutual problem-solving, and professional learning and growth clearly were not part of the agenda.

No work situation is totally negative, and there were two aspects of Karen's that were positive. First, there were professionals in other agencies in the county to which she was assigned who became an important source of support. Other social workers employed by the local CMHC, the schools, and the Department of Social Services frequently worked with Karen because of mutual clients or programs. She had developed close, positive relationships with several of these colleagues, and their acceptance and support helped Karen cope with the problems she faced back at the institution.

The second positive feature in Karen's job was the high degree of autonomy. Karen found that she could modify her role in significant ways without her superiors' knowing or interfering. For instance, if she wanted to deemphasize client contact and direct her energies instead into program development, she could do so. This high degree of autonomy seemed to be the one benefit of the lack of supervision.

Thus, despite some positive aspects, Karen's job generally was filled with stress, frustration, and disappointment. Consequently, her energy and commitment gradually declined over time. At first, she had "big ups and downs": One week she would be depressed and feel that everything was hopeless; two weeks later she would feel ready to try to change the situation to make things better. Eventually, Karen settled into a "survival" mentality. Her agitation and dissatisfaction lessened as she resigned herself to the situation and learned to "live with it." However, she felt a sense of stagnation, as though she were just marking time. She said that she was "looking out" for other job possibilities, but the work situation no longer seemed so bad that she wanted to look actively for another. Karen was more aware than ever that many other jobs could be as bad or worse than this one, and she was conscious of the stresses associated with adjusting to a new job, even a good one. At least in her present job she had come to feel "comfortable."

In her last interview, Karen summed up these feelings—the feelings of burnout—in this way:

> I don't know what my "agenda" is now. I think my agenda right now is just plain survival and perseverance until something else comes along. Yeah, I guess I've concluded that I'm not totally happy in this situation, but I'm not really ready to invest too much to change it. I will just go along at the moment, do what I can where I like to do it, until something else comes along. I keep my ears open as far as other job possibilities; so in a very limited way I'm looking for something else. But it's not bad enough to make me really look. I now have the sense that things here are just stagnant, that what's happening is going to continue to happen and that I'm not getting a real challenge. And I need challenge to be able to grow more. So if I really want to grow, professionally, I've got to get into a different situation. . . . But there's comfort in this job that holds me back from looking for something else.

> (Interviewer: What are the comforts?)

> The fact that I know what's expected of me. I can do the job. I know the people. I'm beginning to know the ropes, and job changing means having to learn whole new expectations again, maybe getting into things that I don't know about. And that's kind of scary. . . . I guess the job's become comfortable, and I really don't like facing that fact. Somehow, just the connotation of being comfortable with the job . . . I don't like that and I don't know why.

A CONTRASTING EXAMPLE

The case of clinical social worker Diane Peterson presents a very different picture. Despite some initial difficulties, her job was stimulating and fulfilling. She found strong supports in the job and from the people she worked with. Consequently, at the point in time when Karen Mikelson was feeling emotionally detached and stagnant, Diane Peterson felt exhilarated and fulfilled. Unlike Karen, Diane looked ahead to a future filled with exciting new possibilities.

Diane Peterson worked in a new, federally funded alcoholism program. The program was relatively small: three other master's-level professionals hired shortly before Diane, and six nonprofessional therapists, most of whom were ex-alcoholics. There were three primary activities associated with Diane's job: individual and group therapy with alcoholics; public education, primarily through lecturing; and consultation and training for other mental health professionals.

The clients with whom she worked directly were not always the most rewarding. In this sense, they had much in common with the mentally retarded clients with whom Karen Mikelson worked. Diane said that many of her clients initially were resistant to treatment, especially those who had been referred by the courts for drunk driving and were going through the program merely to avoid a stiffer sentence. However, working with these clients ultimately proved to be rewarding for several reasons.

First, Diane believed that despite their initial resistance, many of her clients ultimately responded to the lectures and other parts of their program. Second, compared with Karen Mikelson's retarded clients, Diane's functioned at a higher level. They were self-sufficient and many were intelligent, verbal, and capable of self-reflection and insight. Consequently, Diane was able to use her clinical skills and techniques with them, and at some level they usually responded. A third important factor was her case load: there was no pressure for this special federally funded program to take any more clients than they wished to. Consequently, Diane and all of the other workers carried relatively light case loads. The expectation was that a worker would take clients as she felt she needed them.

Despite these many positive aspects of the work with clients, Diane observed that it could be demoralizing to work with alcoholics in treatment all day, every day. Fortunately, the variety built into her job prevented this from occurring. Besides working directly with clients, Diane worked with family members, employers, and other agencies and professionals. She also could mix individual treatment with family and group therapy, lectures and educational presentations, and staff development and consultation. Combined with this variety was an unusually high degree of autonomy: The workers in her agency were able to modify their roles so that they did the things they felt most comfortable doing. Thus, one worker might do more one-to-one counseling and therapy, while another might do more group work or lecturing. Staff were encouraged to expand their roles and competencies, but they were allowed to do so at a rate they felt comfortable with.

Perhaps the most important factor that made this job unusually rewarding was the strong emphasis placed on the personal and professional growth of the staff. It began with orientation. When Diane was hired, she was told, "We know you're probably not ready to start seeing clients right away. There are several things you'll want to learn first." In other words, there was explicit recognition that receiving a professional degree was just the *beginning* of her professional development. During her first two months on the job, Diane worked part-time. She did not have a case load. She was sent to an intensive, week-long training program, during which she attended numerous seminars and lectures and, most important, observed treatment being done by others. When she returned from this week of training, she sat in on interviews conducted by other therapists. When she felt ready, she began seeing clients on her own. She said that this orientation was extremely useful, and she lamented that her training in graduate school had not been nearly so good.

Even after her formal orientation ended, Diane continued to participate in training experiences. All of the staff were encouraged to attend outside workshops and to share what they learned with the others when they returned. Only three months after she began working at the agency, Diane was given permission to enter a year-long training program in alcoholism treatment that required her to be away from her job three days each month. She found the program invaluable and said that it was the "biggest fringe benefit of the job."

This support for professional growth and development for the staff seemed to be part of a more basic attitude of the agency's administration. Diane tried to sum it up when she described her work setting as a "people-oriented" agency. What she meant was that her supervisor and other administrators seemed to be sensitive to and concerned about the emotional and intellectual well-being of their staff, and they trusted the staff and assumed that their commitment to the work was strong and sincere. The emphasis was placed on support rather than control. For example, Diane's supervisor recognized that "time-outs" were necessary in the kind of work she did. Thus, there were no raised eyebrows when Diane had no meetings scheduled for one or two hours at a time. Also, when Diane requested a week off only three months after she had begun her job, the request was granted. The implicit message seemed to be, "You know what is best for you. You will work as hard as you can without our breathing down your neck because you are a dedicated professional." Diane thought that this policy on the part of the administration probably made her and most of the other staff work harder than they would have if the supervision had been less supportive and more controlling and bureaucratic.

This "people-oriented" approach to supervision probably contributed to the high level of sharing and support that characterized relations among the staff. Diane stated that the atmosphere in the office was positive. The staff trusted and respected each other. No one seemed to feel that others were not pulling their weight; no one felt exploited or rejected. Staff members were willing to do things that were not explicitly part of their formal job description; for instance, the professional staff answered the telephones for the secretaries when the secretaries were too busy with other pressing work. Diane summed it up when she described the agency as a "comfortable place to be, a fun place."

Diane was especially close to two other workers in the agency who were hired when she was, and these colleagues were an important source of support. The structure of their jobs allowed them to see each other two or three times each week and all day on Thursdays. They came to know and like each other during the week of training they went through together shortly after being hired. Diane said that they backed each other up "all the time." For instance, if one could not do a lecture she had promised to do, another would do it for her.

Diane recognized that there was much potential for conflict between the professional and paraprofessional clinicians. However, she claimed that in this agency, the professionals uniformly respected the ability of the paraprofessional workers. Everyone seemed to believe that both the professional and paraprofessional had something valuable and unique to offer to alcoholism treatment. Diane observed that there was much mutual give-and-take among the two groups at the agency, and this further contributed to the positive social atmosphere, the collegiality and support that characterized staff interactions.

Just as Karen Mikelson's job was not all negative, so Diane Peterson's was not all positive. One major source of stress and difficulty was a misunderstanding initially concerning the nature of her role. Staff at a family counseling agency where she was supposed to spend part of each week thought she would start sooner than she did. This agency also began using her as a crisis worker which was inconsistent with the way that her supervisor in the alcoholism agency wanted her to function. Diane also had difficulty in getting staff at the family counseling agency to attend the training sessions on alcoholism that she offered. Fortunately, the directors of the two agencies finally met with Diane and worked out the differences in their conceptions of her role. When this role conflict was resolved, much tension was relieved.

The second shortcoming of her job was not so easily rectified. Diane had been hired under a federal grant, and problems in the administration of the grant and the application for refunding made her job precarious. This lack of job security was a major source of stress for Diane, as she had no control over the situation. The decision ultimately would be made in Washington, and it apparently would depend on political and bureaucratic considerations that Diane and others at the agency could not control, predict, or even fully comprehend. Diane said that this uncertainty concerning refunding and the status of her job was a major source of anxiety for her and several other workers.

Fortunately, the support that staff in this unusual work setting received from each other and from the organization helped them cope with the pressures and uncertainties that could not be prevented. Consequently, after eight months, Diane was more committed and enthusiastic about her work than she had been when she had started. In fact, at one point she contrasted her work role with her role as a mother: As a mother, she felt that she gave and gave, getting nothing in return. But in her work, she believed that she constantly got something in return. She said that she enjoyed her job "immensely." She had become "fascinated" by the problem of alcoholism and wanted to stay and make a career in the field. In our last interview, she summed up her involvement as follows:

> One has to start realizing, "Am I going to make this a 9–5 job, or am I prepared to give an awful lot more of myself?" I'm really seeing now that my hobby is my job. It involves reading more and just being involved more. This is a whole way of life. It's not just a job. I read journals in the bathtub. In bed I read the newest pamphlet that just came out on alcoholism. I guess I enjoy it. It's not like school. I often feel that I'm doing this because I want to, not because I have to.

WHAT MADE THE DIFFERENCE?

In considering these two work experiences, it is difficult to imagine two responses to work in the human services that could be more different. Karen Mikelson seemed to epitomize the frustrated, discouraged, demoralized individual whose efforts to improve her work situation are constantly stymied and who eventually settles into an acceptable but stagnating situation. Diane Peterson, on the other hand, represents an unusually positive response to work. She began with little background or interest in the field of alcoholism, and after eight months in a fulfilling job she had decided to make the field her career. What factors seem to account for the difference in these two reactions?

There seemed to be several differences in the work situations that could account for the differences in these workers' reactions, many of which related to *a sense of impact and control* over one's work situation. Karen Mikelson worked in a large, state-operated facility. Many of the rules and policies were set by bureaucrats sitting in offices at the state capital. As a social worker, Karen was part of a particularly marginal and powerless group within the setting. The institution was bureaucratic in the classical sense: there were numerous detailed rules and regulations defining what one could and could not do, and supervisory personnel regarded many of those rules as important and inviolable. Karen's supervision, especially during her

first months on the job, was close and controlling. She was expected
to discuss many of the things she did with her supervisor.

On the other hand, Diane Peterson worked in a relatively small,
independent agency. The agency was dependent on the federal government for its funding, and this imposed certain restrictions; but it
was much more autonomous than the state-run facility for which
Karen Mikelson worked. The agency's "locus of control" was much
greater in Diane's case. Also, as a social worker, Diane was part of the
highest status group within the setting, and the power structure of her
agency was informal and collegial rather than formal and bureaucratic. There were few rigid rules and restrictions imposed on the
workers by a mistrustful and controlling administration.

These differences in the nature of organizational and individual
power were perhaps best demonstrated by the way in which disturbing role conflicts were handled. Both Diane and Karen received
conflicting role messages initially. However, in Diane's situation, the
two role senders who created the conflict responded to her complaints, met, and resolved the conflict. In contrast, Karen felt helpless in her attempts to resolve the conflict. The two role senders
refused to discuss their differences, and the conflict ultimately was
resolved only when one of the parties quit.

The differences in *clientele and case loads* also influenced the
relative sense of impact and control experienced by these two mental
health workers. Karen Mikelson had a large case load comprised of
clients who were functioning at low levels. Consequently, she believed there was little she could do to improve their functioning.
Diane Peterson not only had a small case load, but she controlled its
size. Her clients generally functioned at a higher level than did
Karen's. This difference in the clientele not only provided Diane with
a greater sense of impact and efficacy; it also allowed her to use her
clinical skills to a much greater extent. The verbal, intelligent client
living in an intact family allowed her to do "real" treatment. Her role
was more consistent with her professional identity.

The two work settings also differed in the opportunities they provided for *learning new skills and perspectives*. There was a strong
emphasis on training and professional development in Diane's agency
that was totally lacking in Karen's institution. The differences in the

orientation each received typified this more general difference in institutional priorities. Diane's setting also encouraged *experimentation and innovation* to a much greater degree. In fact, Diane worked in *a setting that was new* and part of a field that was beginning to grow in popularity. After many years of neglect, alcoholism was receiving new support from the government and the mental health professions. Diane's agency represented the new ideas that were guiding work in the area. Consequently, Diane saw herself as part of a new and exciting "crusade," full of hopes and possibilities. The future was bright for her field and the kind of work her agency did. Karen Mikelson, on the other hand, worked in an old, established setting that was generally regarded as obsolete. There was a growing belief that the large institution for the retarded had been a mistake. The primary objective now was to get clients out of the institution and close it down as soon as possible. Maintaining enthusiasm and commitment to one's work in such a setting clearly was difficult.

Relations with co-workers was the last area in which there were important differences. The level of interpersonal and intergroup conflict was much lower in Diane's setting. Staff generally regarded one another with trust and respect. There were more opportunities for supportive interaction among the staff. They were less isolated from one another physically as well as psychologically. Not surprisingly, Diane came to feel that she could rely on her co-workers for help if she needed it. In Karen's setting, the only thing that united the social work staff was their sense of a "common enemy" in their medically dominated setting.

Thus, despite many similarities in their training and personal backgrounds, these two human service professionals differed in their response to their work; and there were numerous differences in the work settings that contributed to the difference in response. Although personality structure, knowledge, and skill may have played a role, the work setting seemed to be crucial. This analysis of two actual work experiences suggests some of the factors that influence job stress and burnout more generally in the human services.

Chapter 5

THE "ORGANIZATIONAL DESIGN" AS A SOURCE OF BURNOUT

The "organizational design" of a human service program is an important factor in the motivation and performance of staff (Cherniss, 1980b, 1980c). By organizational design, I mean the formal, rational properties of an organization that can be readily controlled by those responsible for designing and/or managing a program. Three components of organizational design that are particularly important are the role structure, the power structure, and the normative structure.

THE ROLE STRUCTURE'S IMPACT ON BURNOUT

One of the most important ways in which the work setting influences job stress and burnout is through the role structure (Cherniss, 1980b). Role structure is referred to here as the way tasks and duties are allocated among specified roles in a setting. There are many different ways this can be done; thus, there are many different possible role structures. Certain role structures will tend to create more stress and strain than will others. Certain role structures will tend to provide more stimulation and greater individual involvement and satisfaction than will others. Thus, the role structure of a human service program ultimately will influence the severity of staff burnout.

To appreciate how the role structures of human service programs can vary, consider as an example a halfway house for emotionally disturbed adults. In such a program, one could identify dozens, if not hundreds, of specific tasks that must be performed for the program to function. Each room must be cleaned periodically. Meals must be cooked and prepared. Counseling or therapy may be the treatment modality; if so, someone must do it. Contacts with family, employers, and other community agencies must be established and maintained.

Although the staff in one of these halfway houses might assume that there are only certain ways of dividing responsibility for these various tasks, the possible "universe of alternatives" probably is much greater than they imagine (Sarason, 1972). For instance, a special role ("cook") might be created for meal preparation and related tasks. Or preparing the meals might be considered a responsibility of the regular staff, to be performed along with other duties such as counseling and group supervision. Still another possibility is that the residents themselves would cook their meals. Similar alternatives could be identified for virtually any other program task or function.

Unfortunately, the role structure of a human service program usually is not designed with the prevention of job stress and burnout as a major consideration. Thus, frequently the role structure produces strain in certain staff roles in the program. Previous research and theory have suggested several specific characteristics of a role that contribute to job stress and strain, including role conflict, role ambiguity, and the amount of challenge, variety, and autonomy available in the role. In terms of the theoretical framework presented in Chapter 3, these role characteristics create an imbalance between resources and demands. In some cases, demands exceed resources. In other cases, resources exceed demands, and there is a lack of stimulation. In either case, the role player's efforts to achieve psychological success and a sense of efficacy are thwarted by the work setting's role structure.

Role Conflict and Ambiguity

In an important series of studies, Kahn and his co-workers (1964) found that role conflict and role ambiguity were two factors in work settings that contribute to stress, strain, and the emotional detachment that we have referred to as burnout. Although not specifically concerned with human service organizations, Kahn's ideas are clearly relevant to these types of settings.

"Role overload" probably is the most obvious type of conflict experienced by staff in human service programs. The demands tied to the role exceed the role player's time and effort. An example is the social worker in one program who was responsible for coordinating after-care services for over 200 ex-hospital patients. Responsibility for 20 such clients would begin to strain her capacity to perform adequately; a case load of 200 made it impossible to function effectively. In such a role, one can at best be effective with only a small percentage of one's case load. One must learn to live with the fact that inadequate care will be given to most of those for whom one is responsible. Given the importance of efficacy and psychological success in human service work (see Chapter 3), one would expect that role overload thus would represent a major source of burnout.

Role overload also should contribute to increased stress and burnout because of its impact on coping. McGrath (1970) observed that effective coping with stress requires time for its accomplishment. Whether the coping involves a search for information, direct action, or even palliation, there will be an optimal length of time for the coping to occur. If there is not adequate time due to the constant instrusion of new demands, coping will be disrupted. The individual will tend to fall back on more primitive, less effective, more psychologically defensive coping behaviors. Thus, if there is a high degree of role overload in a job and few structured "time outs" when one can escape from role demands and "work through" the demands that already have been made (Maslach, 1976), emotional exhaustion and burnout are more likely.

Research studies have confirmed the existence of a relationship between role overload and burnout. For instance, a study of child abuse programs found that the size of the case load was strongly correlated with staff burnout rates (Berkeley Planning Associates, 1977). However, the researchers found that a relatively large increase in the case load was necessary before the burnout rate was affected, suggesting that responsibility for more clients by itself does not contribute to burnout until the increase exceeds the staff member's resources.

A study of new professionals employed in public human service agencies also found a relationship between work load and burnout (Cherniss, 1980a). When the most burned-out subjects were compared with those who were most resistant to burnout, it was found that the typical work loads of the burned-out subjects were much heavier. Similarly, a study of 845 Social Security Administration employees found a correlation between large case loads and burnout (Barad, 1979). Thus, as one would expect, role overload seems to be a source of job stress and burnout in the human services.

Occasionally, role conflict involves not too many demands (overload) but demands that are inherently incompatible. The role occupant is sent two messages, and he or she cannot comply with one without disobeying the other. A good example of this situation involved one of the clinical social workers described in the last chapter, Diane Peterson. Although she was hired and paid by the local Council on Alcoholism, she was assigned to work in a family service agency part-time. The council told her that she was only to work with clients who have alcoholism-related problems, and she was to do so in collaboration with a regular staff member of the family service agency in order to increase their expertise in this area. However, the staff and director at the family service agency saw Diane as simply another staff member. Not only was she expected to work alone with her clients, but she even was assigned to do general intake like any other staff member. When her boss at the council heard that she was doing intake and that cases were being "dumped" on her, he told her that she was not performing the role as intended and should change her role at the family service agency as soon as possible.

Eventually, the heads of the two agencies met with the social workers and ironed out their differences. However, until they did so, this social worker was caught in the middle. Because she received conflicting role demands from her supervisors and co-workers, she experienced considerable stress and strain. She could not please one set of role senders without displeasing the other.

In the above example, the situation involved "inter-sender role conflict" (Kahn et al., 1964): The conflicting role messages came from different role senders. Sometimes, however, the conflicting messages come from the same role sender, a situation referred to as "intra-sender role conflict." An example would be a juvenile probation officer who is expected to be both a rehabilitation counselor and an agent of social control. Although it may be possible to do both effectively, usually one's attempts to control and punish a youth will compromise one's ability to develop the trust necessary for effective personal counseling. Classroom teachers who are expected to maintain class control and also generate a love for learning in their students encounter a similar conflict.

Another type of role conflict that contributes to stress and burnout in human service settings is "person-role conflict." Here, the conflict is more internal; the role requires certain behavior that is inconsistent with the role player's motives, abilities, or moral values. An all-too-common example in human service settings is the plight of the clinician who is asked to do mental health consultation in another community setting. Typically, clinical social workers, psychologists, and psychiatrists are trained in psychodiagnostics and therapy. They receive little, if any, training in mental health consultation. Thus, when they are assigned to do mental health consultation, they feel unprepared to do so because they lack the necessary knowledge and skills. This is an example of person-role conflict, and it can be another major source of job stress.[1]

In fact, one distinctive feature of many human service jobs is that they require professionals to work with new populations in new ways. Unless the staff are adequately trained for these new role demands, the consequences will be high levels of person-role conflict, job stress, dissatisfaction, and burnout.

Of course, professionals have a tendency to resolve this type of person-role conflict by changing the problem into one they can solve. There is an old anecdote which illustrates this point: A patient went to see a physician about an ailment, and, despite a thorough examination, the physician could not figure out what was wrong. He thought for a moment, and then said to the patient, "I want you to go home and do the following: three times a day, open the window wide and breathe deeply." The patient answered, "But doctor, it's the middle of winter, and it's freezing outside. If I do what you tell me, I'll catch pneumonia." "Precisely," the physician said. "When you've caught pneumonia, come back to see me again. Then I'll know what you have and how to take care of it!" Staff in human service programs frequently must feel like the physician in this story: They are asked to deal with problems they are unfamiliar with which require interventions they have never been trained to perform.

Given our prèvious discussion of the importance of feeling competent and efficacious in work (Chapter 3), one would predict that this type of role conflict would be particularly stressful. If helpers believe they lack the ability to achieve success, they are likely to experience a "crisis of competence" that can be disruptive psychologically (Cherniss, 1980a). Skill, knowledge, and ability are critical resources for meeting job demands in the human services. When helpers lack those resources, one would expect considerable stress and burnout.

These considerations suggest that particular kinds of clients will tend to be identified as sources of burnout more than other types, but the source of the problem is really not the client. Research on the relationship between client contact and burnout in human service settings has produced conflicting results. Sarata (1974) found that in institutions for the mentally retarded greater client contact was associated with more job dissatisfaction. However, Cherniss and Egnatios (1978a) found just the opposite trend in their study of community mental health programs. Apparently this discrepancy was due to the difference in the client populations *and* the extent to which the providers believed they had the skills necessary for successful intervention. Clients who tend to be more resistant (such as adolescents) and/ or less successful (such as the mentally retarded, after-care clients, drug addicts, or individuals with severe character disorders) will create more stress in their providers. This will occur especially in those situations where the providers must spend most of their time with these less rewarding clients, without opportunities to work with more rewarding ones. The source of stress and burnout in this instance is person-role conflict: The worker usually lacks the skills or other resources necessary to "reach" the client. Sometimes there are "breakthroughs," but frequently the worker goes for long periods without seeing any perceptible signs of success.

Sometimes, person-role conflict involves the individual's motives, values, and goals rather than (or in addition to) abilities. I recently talked to a graduate student who described herself as a "casualty of burnout." She had been working as a therapist in a CMHC for three years before she quit in frustration and returned to graduate school. She said that one of the greatest sources of dissatisfaction and strain was the role she was expected to assume in working with clients. At this particular CMHC, therapists were expected to be "generalists." This meant that if a client needed temporary housing, the therapist was expected to help the client secure it. If the client lost his job, the therapist was expected to help the client get it back or find a new one. In other words, the therapist was expected to do much more than therapy; and for this particular individual, this expectation was the cause of much "person-role" conflict. She wanted to do "therapy"; while she agreed that performing nonclinical tasks for some clients was necessary, she believed that she possessed the necessary knowledge and skills to provide therapeutic assistance and that someone else, presumably with less education and training than she, should do this nonclinical work. In short, she wanted to function as a specialist, but the role required that she function as a generalist. She claimed that this situation finally led to her burnout and decision to quit.

Although other therapists at this CMHC probably were less bothered about this aspect of their roles, they may have found other aspects of their work were dissonant with their conception of their roles. This conflict between the helper's conception of what his or her role should be and the organization's definition of the role is another potential source of job stress and burnout in human service programs.

A special case of this type of role conflict which frequently occurs in human service programs is "professional-bureaucratic role conflict" (Kramer, 1974; Corwin, 1961; Cherniss, 1980a). Professionally oriented helpers tend to believe in and follow a particular set of norms regarding the helping relationship. These norms constitute the "professional service ideal," and they are an important part of the culture of professionalism. Unfortunately, human service programs are public institutions that tend to be organized along bureaucratic lines, and there are situations in which the professional service ideal comes into conflict with organizational self-interest and the bureaucratic mode of functioning. As numerous writers have observed (Katkin & Sibley, 1973; McIntyre, 1969; Merton, 1940), the bureaucratic mode of organization emphasizes orderliness, standardization, uniformity, efficiency, public accountability, and impersonality. The professional service ideal, on the other hand, emphasizes the uniqueness of the individual, sensitivity to the special needs of each client, flexibility, individual initiative and resourcefulness, and the goal of personal growth and development. Given these two distinct and potentially incompatible conceptions of service delivery, one would expect that professional practitioners who also are *employees* of bureaucratic organizations would experience considerable person-role conflict.

The recent controversy over "Management Information Systems" (MIS) in human service programs is a good example of this conflict between the bureaucratic and professional role orientations. Practitioners tend to oppose introduction of MIS because they seem to threaten the confidentiality and privacy of the client and the professional autonomy and flexibility of the practitioner. However, administrators tend to favor MIS because they will improve efficiency, accountability, planning, and coordination. From the bureaucratic perspective, MIS are attractive; but from the professional perspective, they may be abhorrent. However, when administrators introduce MIS into a program, staff members are expected to cooperate, even though many of them believe this would violate their personal value system. This situation may generate much organizational conflict, stress, and burnout.

However, even without the introduction of MIS and other accountability mechanisms, the potential for professional-bureaucratic role conflict exists in any human service organization. This potential is demonstrated well by an example suggested by Kramer (1974). Although the setting is a medical hospital, similar situations could be found in any program:

A nurse has been closely watching a post-operative patient whose psychological depression has been impeding his recovery. For days he has been silently brooding, unresponsive to all efforts to make contact with him. Finally, one evening he begins to respond to the nurse, talking about his worries and concerns for the first time. As she sits with him, listening sympathetically, using all of her interpersonal skills to support his emotional catharsis, she feels that this is one of those rare and precious moments when she is really "doing nursing" in the way she was trained.

Unfortunately, just after the patient began talking, the dinner trays came up from the kitchens. It is dinner time, the food is getting cold, the other patients are hungry and restless. Organizational efficiency requires that patients be fed at a certain time. But if the nurse leaves her patient to serve dinner to the others, the patient may withdraw into his shell again. The optimal time for talking to an emotionally troubled surgery patient cannot be regimented, controlled, or even predicted.

As this example suggests, there will be times when the needs of particular clients will conflict with the needs or demands of the organization, and the staff member is the one caught in the middle. Furthermore, one cannot always argue that the client's needs are more legitimate than the organization's, for many organizational rules and procedures were created in order to better serve the clientele. In the above example, staying with the depressed patient could adversely affect the nutrition, health, and morale of other patients. Thus, there often is no easy solution to these role conflicts, and they are the source of job-related stress in many types of human service settings.

As human service personnel move away from their own setting and work with others, the problem of professional-bureaucratic role conflict becomes even more prevalent and frustrating. As consultants or educators, human service staff often must reconcile their goals and values with those of systems that are indifferent, if not hostile, to mental health concerns. A good example of this situation was an incident described by a public health nurse who was asked to conduct a sex education program in a public school. She soon found that her professional judgment concerning what was needed for an effective program was summarily ignored by school personnel. Not only was

she forced to compromise her professional standards, but she also felt
that she was treated as an insignificant pawn, increasing her sense of
helplessness and frustration:

> The principal mentioned to me about a growing-up program, so I went
> down and talked to the teachers who were going to be involved in it,
> and I kind of set up a date and I told him the date. He wanted it the first
> week in May, so I went ahead and ordered the film. Okay, I walk in
> there last week and he says to me, "Well, we set up the program for
> Wednesday evening at 7:30," just like, "Okay you do this, this, and
> this." And I looked at him and I . . . First of all, fifth and sixth grade
> boys and girls in two hours? He's crazy! You know, there's no way. I
> said, "First of all, we need more time than that," and he says, "Well,
> we've gone for two years like that," and I said, "Well, I know how
> much time I need to spend with these people, because they have a lot
> of questions. Fifth and sixth grade kids know a lot; they're doing a lot
> of things that we weren't doing." And this man says to me, "Well, if
> they have questions, they can go home and ask their parents," and I
> said, "Well, what's the purpose of doing this? The reason that we do it
> is because parents don't do it at home." He said, "Well, I don't know if
> I agree with that," and I said, "Well what's the whole philosophy of
> education?" I got into a big discussion with him. We were out in the
> hall and I was just burning. I just had had it. He was putting me down
> . . . I guess he might have been in a lousy mood because he is kind of
> temperamental, kind of dictatorial. That school is run like the Army,
> or something. He's really strict. His secretary jumps when he says
> something. You know, he likes to control people like that, so I under-
> stand that personality. But you know, here I am, I don't work for the
> Board of Education. I'm a resource person [Cherniss, 1980a].

Although this nurse saw the conflict primarily in terms of personality, in fact, what was at issue was more fundamental. The nurse
saw herself as a professional who was providing a service to the
students. They were her clients, not the principal or the school.
However, the school system saw her as a public employee under the
principal's jurisdiction when she was working in *his* school. The
principal was simply a representative of the school system in this
conflict. Although such clashes clearly are influenced by "personality" factors, the conflict between the professional conception of ser-

vice delivery and the bureaucratic conception makes such clashes inevitable. When they occur, the helper's professional autonomy and self-esteem are threatened, contributing to stress and burnout.

The stress associated with professional-bureaucratic role conflict also is particularly severe because autonomy is a strong motive for choosing a professional career, and bureaucratic interference is unexpected (More & Kohn, 1966; Sarason et al., 1975). New professionals simply are not prepared for the large amount of work that was not part of the "psychological contract" (Schein, 1971) when they entered the field. What Lortie (1966) said about new lawyers tends to be true of those who enter other professions as well: Their image of professional work is charismatic, not routine. They see themselves working in a special, isolated, pure situation consisting only of their clients and themselves. Even when they anticipate working in a large bureaucratic system such as a community mental health program, their image of what professional work will be like does not change dramatically. Consequently, the "reality shock" that they experience during the first part of their career is strong, and professional-bureaucratic role conflict is a significant element in that shaky transition from student to professional (Kramer, 1974; Cherniss, 1980a).

To summarize, role conflict is a major source of stress and burnout in human service programs. Several different types of role conflict have been identified, including role overload, inter-sender role conflict, intra-sender role conflict, and person-role conflict. When role demands are inconsistent with either a helper's abilities or goals, values, and beliefs, internal conflict and stress are produced. A particularly prevalent type of conflict found in human service programs is professional-bureaucratic role conflict, generated by the attempt to merge two potentially incompatible role orientations: the professional and the bureaucratic.

Role ambiguity is a second major type of role strain identified by Kahn et al. (1964). Role ambiguity occurs when the role player lacks the information necessary for adequate performance of the role. For instance, to return to the example of the social worker employed in an after-care program, the role strain would be even greater if the records left by the previous social worker were incomplete and inaccurate. Unfortunately, those employed in the human services frequently must work in highly ambiguous situations, and thus some role strain is inevitable. However, work settings within the human service field also will vary in the degree to which role ambiguity pervades the setting.

Another example of role ambiguity occurred in a group home for emotionally disturbed adolescents. The staff in this program also suffered from role overload; during any given shift, they were supposed to do more than time allowed. Fortunately, the supervisor recognized the realities of the situation and told the staff that it was all right if they did not manage to do everything as long as the "important" things got done. However, during one staff meeting, the staff complained that they were not sure what the supervisor considered the "important" things. It soon became obvious that until this issue was clarified, the staff would experience high levels of role ambiguity and strain. After some discussion about program priorities, much of the ambiguity was disspelled. The supervisor and some staff then formed a task group which prepared a checklist indicating what tasks should be performed on a typical shift and the relative importance of each. This intervention seemed to be effective in reducing role ambiguity for staff in this program.

In their study of role conflict and ambiguity in organizations, Kahn et al. (1964) identified six specific sources of role ambiguity that can contribute to strain:

(1) information concerning the scope and responsibilities of a job;
(2) information about co-workers' expectations;
(3) information required to perform the job adequately;
(4) information about opportunities for advancement;
(5) information about supervisors' evaluations;
(6) information about what is happening in the organization.

According to Kahn et al., the degree to which work in different fields is ambiguous along these dimensions varies. The ambiguity of jobs within a work setting also varies considerably. Roles that are highly ambiguous on several of these dimensions will contribute to high levels of stress, strain, and burnout in those who occupy them.

Unfortunately, there are many sources of role ambiguity inherent in human service work. Several were noted in Chapter 3. They include lack of clear feedback concerning the results of one's work, ambiguous goals and criteria for performance (such as the goal of "psychological growth"), the long and uncertain time perspective necessary for results to become visible, and the problem of "authorship"—that is, not knowing whether a helper's efforts were responsible for positive change in a client when change does occur. Even the methods used in the human services are surrounded with ambiguity. For instance, despite hundreds of studies, controversy concerning the efficacy of psychotherapy still exists. There is no clear-cut evidence that psychotherapy is better than "benign neglect." Similarly, the superiority of one therapeutic school (for example, transactional analysis, behavior modification, or psychoanalysis) over another cannot be established conclusively. Thus, the mental health practitioner inevitably must work in a dense cognitive "fog." Role ambiguity is a way of life. However, as we have seen, the role structure of the work setting can reduce or increase the role ambiguity in which the practitioner must work. The greater the ambiguity, the greater the stress and potential for burnout.

Given both the prevalence of role ambiguity in human service work and its adverse psychological effects, one would expect that staff would identify this as a major source of job dissatisfaction. Confirmation comes from a study by Cherniss and Egnatios (1978a). They asked staff to indicate the three major sources of dissatisfaction and satisfaction in their work. The responses were coded and content-analyzed. The findings showed that the major source of dissatisfaction was related to role ambiguity: Specifically, the respondents wrote down items such as "poor communication," "lack of order and organization," and "ambiguity." Role ambiguity also emerged as an important source of burnout in child abuse agencies (Berkeley Planning Associates, 1977). In fact, the perceived amount and clarity of communication in these settings was the second strongest predictor of staff burnout (quality of leadership was the strongest predictor). Job clarity, another measure of role ambiguity used in this study, also was correlated with burnout. Thus, research confirms that role ambiguity is an important source of stress and dissatisfaction in the human services.

To summarize, the role structure of a human service program

affects job-related stress through its impact on role conflict and ambiguity. Role conflict and ambiguity make it difficult for workers to adequately meet the demands associated with their jobs; consequently, they find it impossible to achieve psychological success in their work. If the worker is not able to alter the work situation and reduce the role conflict and ambiguity, his sense of helplessness ultimately may lead to a pattern of emotional withdrawal.

Opportunities for Stimulation and Meaning

The second major way in which a program's role structure may contribute to burnout is through its impact on the "motivating potential of the job." By this I mean the extent to which the job is stimulating and meaningful. In Chapter 3, I noted that insufficient stimulation can be as stressful as too much stimulation, especially when the person feels he or she has no control over the amount of stimulation. For many individuals who work in the human services the main problem is not overload, conflict, or ambiguity, but *boredom*. Their work lives lack challenge, variety, and meaning.

Previous research on the motivating potential of the job by Hackman and Oldham (1975) suggested that when work lacks challenge and stimulation, the worker's involvement and motivation suffer. They have identified a number of "job design factors" that seem to affect the motivating potential of a job. Research studies involving mental retardation and mental health programs (Sarata, 1974; Sarata & Jeppesen, 1977) have found that these job design factors discriminate among staff roles and are associated with differences in satisfaction, morale, and involvement in work.

One of the most important job design factors is *variety*. Although a staff member in a human service program undoubtedly enjoys more variety in his or her job than does an assembly-line worker in an automobile factory, the difference is only relative. Large differences in the amount of job variety exist *within* the human services, and research suggests that these differences are associated with burnout.

There are at least two important ways in which the role structure of a human service program influences the amount of variety associated with any particular staff role: the number of different tasks performed, and the number of client groups with which one works on a typical day (Sarata & Jeppesen, 1977). Thus, a staff member who only teaches basket-weaving to after-care patients during a typical day would lack variety compared with another staff member who does various types of counseling with various types of clients, interspersed with supervision and program development activities. The first staff member is locked into a less stimulating job and is more likely to become bored and burned out. In their study of child care agencies, Sarata and Jeppesen (1977) found that variety was more strongly associated with job satisfaction than any other job design factor considered.

A second important job design factor that influences the amount of meaning and stimulation in the job is *task identity*. In the human services, task identity refers to the worker's understanding of how his or her role contributes to the total rehabilitation effort. In some settings, the rehabilitation process is fragmented, with several different staff members involved in different aspects of the process. In other settings, a single staff member is responsible for most of the services provided to the client. As an example, consider two group homes for youth. In the first, each youth is assigned to a child care worker who is the primary therapist for that youth. The child care worker conducts all of the counseling sessions which are the primary mode of treatment. The same worker also meets regularly with the youth's family and attempts to effect necessary change in the family system. The same worker also consults with the youth's teachers and employer. In the second group home, the child care workers *share* responsibility for the care of the youth in the setting; no individual assignments are made. Individual therapy is provided by a psychiatrist. Work with the family is done by a social worker. A special school liason worker is responsible for consultation with teachers. In these examples, the task identity for a child care worker would be much greater in the first home. One would expect that the child care workers in that home would feel more involved with the clients. Their work would seem more meaningful and stimulating. Consequently, burnout in child care workers should be lower in the first home.

It also should be clear from these examples, however, that the job design factors are interrelated. Child care workers in the first home experience more variety as well as more task identity. Also, the advantages associated with greater variety or task identity may be canceled out by increased role conflict or ambiguity. For instance, if the child care workers in the first home are responsible for too many youths, their high variety and high task identity role will overtax their resources. If the work load is not carefully monitored and controlled, increases in the motivating potential of a human service job may create role overload, which makes job stress and burnout more likely. Variety and task identity are advantageous only when role conflict is manageable.

Learning is a third job design factor that contributes to stimulation and meaning in a job. In some work situations, there are many opportunities to acquire new skills and to further one's theoretical sophistication both on and off the job. In other work situations, there are virtually no opportunities. In their study of child care settings, Sarata and Jeppesen (1977) found that learning was one of the three job design factors most strongly correlated with job satisfaction (variety and information were the other two).

In human service work, helpers often feel that they are *giving* constantly and *getting* very little in return. This imbalance is a source of dissatisfaction which exacerbates job stress and burnout. However, when helpers believe they are learning and growing professionally in their work, they begin to perceive that they are getting as well as giving.

It is difficult to feel bored in a job when one is constantly learning. Boredom develops when one has mastered a particular role but must continue to perform it, day after day, year after year. When the role structure of a program allows staff to learn new skills, further their theoretical sophistication, and *use* these new skills and sophistication in their work, the job remains stimulating. Boredom and burnout are prevented.

The importance of learning in human service work can best be conveyed by contrasting the two mental health professionals described in Chapter 4. Karen Mikelson's supervision focused on administrative issues. There was no encouragement for her to *think* about what she was doing. The theory and philosophy of community care were never discussed. Skills that might contribute to greater effectiveness in the role were never identified and taught. There was no encouragement or opportunity to expand the role in order to learn and use new skills such as mental health consultation. Not surprisingly, this social worker soon felt understimulated and bored in her job. Her motivation and involvement dropped quickly after six months, and she began seeking employment elsewhere. Although there clearly were other factors contributing to burnout in this situation, lack of opportunity for learning was an important one.

An underlying assumption of Diane Peterson's program was that traditionally trained health professionals must learn many new skills and conceptual frameworks necessary for effective treatment of alcoholism. Thus, all new staff in this program went through an extensive orientation program. Through this program, they learned much about alcoholism and various treatment techniques. Gradually, the staff began to take on treatment cases. However, they continued to participate in a two-day training retreat every month. Weekly case conferences were used to further sharpen and expand the staff's skills. They also began consulting with and teaching professionals in other agencies and community groups. These experiences further contributed to their learning and intellectual stimulation. Finally, it was expected that the staff would supplement their training by reading relevant journals and books; they were given time during the day to do this, and there were regular opportunities for them to discuss what they had learned with one another. In this case, motivation and involvement substantially increased during the first six months of employment. Originally, Diane Peterson had taken the job in large part because of location, salary, vacation benefits, and hours; she had had little previous background or interest in the area of alcoholism. However, after six months in this intellectually stimulating environment, she had become "hooked" on the field and planned to make it her career. Again, the amount of learning provided by the job seemed to significantly influence the worker's psychological involvement in her work.

Two other job design factors that influence the motivating potential of the job already have been discussed in relationship to role ambiguity; they are *feedback* and *information*. Sarata and Jeppesen (1977) suggested that there are two important sources of feedback in human service settings: supervisory evaluations and information concerning client progress. Important kinds of information include deci-sions which affect the staff member's work, current activities and policies in other parts of the institution, and information about other institutions. In discussing role ambiguity, I suggested that feedback and information are critical "resources," without which a worker cannot adequately perform his or her role and achieve psychological success. Feedback and information also contribute to greater stimula-tion and meaning. If a helper does not receive frequent feedback and is not knowledgeable about the setting in which she is working, the job loses a sense of purpose; it becomes routine, meaningless, and boring. Thus, feedback and information contribute to stimulation at the same time they reduce ambiguity and the potential for failure.

However, increased feedback is not beneficial when it is selec-tively *negative,* and this often is the case in human service work. Sarata and Jeppesen (1977), to their surprise, found no correlation between amount of feedback and job satisfaction in human service workers; in fact, there was a slight negative correlation, though it failed to reach statistical significance. In discussing this finding, they suggested that feedback in this type of work, when it occurs, tends to be negative. When staff receive clear evaluative feedback from su-pervisors, it usually concerns something they did wrong. When staff learn about how their clients are doing, it usually is because the clients are not doing well. Thus, it is easy to see why the feedback that usually occurs in human service work is a mixed blessing.

However, the potential benefits of feedback have been demonstrat-ed in a more recent study by Maslach and Jackson (1978). Using a measure of burnout rather than job satisfaction, they found a signifi-cant negative correlation between the amount of feedback provided in the job and the degree of burnout in 91 mental health and social service workers. Thus, while feedback may not always be positive for the human service worker, it does seem to be associated with lower levels of burnout.

As I noted above, the job design factors associated with stimula-tion and meaning are greatly influenced by the role structure of a program. Previous research has suggested that some roles in a pro-gram are consistently more stimulating than others. For instance, Sarata and Jeppesen (1977) found that staff in administrative roles in agencies serving children enjoyed significantly higher levels of variety, task identity, feedback, learning, information, autonomy, and participation compared with staff in nonadministrative roles. These researchers also found a relationship between professional status and job design: Professional staff perceived significantly higher levels of these job design factors than did nonprofessionals. Thus, professional status as well as role influence the amount of stimulation and meaning available in a job.

To summarize, the role structure of a human service program is an important potential source of job stress and burnout. The way tasks are assigned to roles may contribute to more or less role conflict and ambiguity. The role structure also may contribute to more or less stimulation and meaning through its impact on variety, task identity, and learning. In any human service program, therefore, the optimal role structure is one which minimizes role conflict and ambiguity while maximizing variety, task identity, and learning. Through the role structure, program planners and administrators can increase the staff's sense of efficacy and the amount of stimulation and meaning provided by the work, reducing the incidence of burnout.

THE POWER STRUCTURE'S IMPACT ON BURNOUT

The second major aspect of organizational design that influences burnout is the power structure. Just as there are numerous tasks to be performed in a human service program, so also are there numerous decisions to be made.[2] Any decision affecting a staff person's work may be made by that staff person alone (autonomous decision-making), by that staff person with a group of other persons (collective decision-making), or by a supervisory person or group (hierarchical decision-making). Previous research and theory suggest that hierarchical decision-making may increase job stress and burnout in human service settings.

Helplessness is a major contributor to the stress and maladaptive coping associated with burnout. Although many factors influence the extent to which staff in a program feel helpless, clearly, the degree to which they are able to exercise power and control over their work settings will be a salient one. When the power structure provides for a high degree of autonomous and collective decision-making, the staff will exercise more control over the reinforcers affecting their work than would be the case in a more hierarchical structure. Hierarchical power structures reduce staff autonomy and control, contributing to learned helplessness and burnout.

Several studies have confirmed this proposition. Pearlin (1967) found that dissatisfaction and alienation in nurses were influenced by the extent to which the nurse could influence formal sources of power. Specifically, he found that alienation increased as the positional distance between superior and subordinates increased. The lower a nurse's status in the organization and the greater the number of layers between a nurse and the organizational leadership, the greater the alienation. Physical accessibility and visibility of superiors also were related to alienation, presumably because more accessible and visible superiors could be more easily influenced by the nurses. Pearlin also found that the greater the opportunity for promotion (and thus increased power and responsibility), the less alienation there was in the nursing staff. Thus, all of the factors that influenced the potential organizational power of the nurses were associated with the degree to which they were psychologically involved in their work.

A study by Aiken and Hage (1966) found that staff alienation in 16 social welfare agencies was associated with the degree of *centralization* and *formalization*. Centralization refers, in that study, to the degree to which members at lower levels participated in decision-making. Formalization was the degree to which work was standardized and the amount of deviation from those standards that was allowed. Clearly, in settings where there was a high degree of centralization and formalization, staff power was greatly reduced. In such settings, alienation was high.

More support for the importance of staff autonomy and participation in human service programs came from a study of child abuse programs. This study suggested that the more "bureaucratic" the setting was, the greater the incidence of burnout (Berkeley Planning Associates, 1977). Specifically, the study indicated that measures of bureaucratization, including the degree of innovation allowed, the degree of rule formalization, the amount of autonomy enjoyed by the staff members, and the amount of paperwork and "red tape" in the program, were associated with rates of burnout.

Another study that documented the consequences of bureaucratic interference involved a community reentry program for adult offenders. Sarata and Reppucci (1975) found that when the program was threatened with termination of its funding, a central office investigation, and partial merger with another program, staff became more punitive and authoritarian toward clients, clients were rated as more aggressive, and client distrust increased.

A direct association between autonomy and burnout also emerged from a study of 845 Social Security Administration employees by Barad (1979). In this study, low autonomy was associated with high scores on both the Emotional Exhaustion and Depersonalization subscales of the Maslach Burnout Inventory (Maslach & Jackson, 1978).

Unfortunately, many systemic factors contribute to bureaucratic constraint and lack of autonomy for staff employed in human service programs. These programs frequently receive funding from, and are accountable to, numerous external institutions at the federal, state, and local levels.[3] Arbitrary decisions by any of these outside agencies, based on political or organizational factors rather than client service needs, can disrupt a program and contribute to a sense of dissatisfaction and helplessness in staff. These decisions occur daily in human service programs. They include (1) the arbitrary transfer of staff from one program to another; (2) arbitrary and sudden changes in staff duties and responsibilities; (3) layoffs due to reorganizations; and (4) uncertainty about funding (Dehlinger & Perlman, 1978). Each of these situations represents an instance in which the staff's autonomy and control are restricted.

The critical importance of autonomy and organizational control for human service staff has been demonstrated most clearly and directly in a study by Cherniss and Egnatios (1978b). They asked staff in 22 different community mental health programs to indicate how much influence they had over 11 different types of decisions affecting their work. Staff also indicated how much influence they would *like* to have. For virtually every type of decision, staff wanted significantly more influence than they currently had. Also, the degree of staff autonomy, influence, and control varied with the type of program. Staff in programs serving a more "disturbed" population (for instance, mental retardation, after care, drug abuse, or inpatient programs) enjoyed significantly less autonomy and control. More client contact also was associated with less staff autonomy and participation. Finally, as one would expect, professional staff enjoyed greater autonomy and participation in decision-making than nonprofessional service providers. However, whatever the status or program assignment of the staff, there was a sense of powerlessness. And based on our previous discussion of the dynamics of stress (Chapter 3), one would predict that one's sense of powerlessness would contribute to greater stress and the maladaptive coping pattern associated with learned helplessness and burnout.

The power structure of a program also contributes to stress and burnout indirectly through its impact on the role structure. As I noted above, the role structure of a human service program rarely is designed with the prevention of job stress and burnout in mind. However, if the staff in the affected roles had some control over decisions concerning the role structure, they might well be able to modify their roles in ways that would reduce conflict and ambiguity while increasing challenge and meaning.[4] Thus, a more centralized, hierarchical power structure may lead to greater role conflict and ambiguity and less interesting, stimulating jobs in human service programs.

The psychological impact of low organizational autonomy and control is perhaps best conveyed by the following excerpt from an interview with a clinical social worker employed in a community mental health program. Although this individual may have been unusually sensitive about the issue of autonomy and status, his frustration about his lack of participation was not different from that expressed by other mental health workers whom I have interviewed:

> I was very surprised about how they brought me in. I had no say, almost, in what I would be doing. Like when it came to discussing salaries, they wouldn't talk about it. They said, "This is how much we'll give you for your past experience." Well, it's as if everyone's past experience is equal based on time, not on the actual work or the quality of the work or what projects you were doing; and I thought mine were unusual. And already I felt discounted at this place. They weren't seeing me as an individual. . . . It was almost as if you're a cog. "If we

hire you, this is what you will do." So I was negotiating on what clients I would see, whether I would have families and children, and they would not promise me that. And they knew I was good at it. They said, "Well, we distribute the kids evenly." Well, I thought that's stupid. Like why should everyone see the same number of kids? And so far, I have one child under the age of 12 years old. Out of 14 cases, they've given me one of what I want. And I'm not satisfied with that [Cherniss, 1980a].

This person hoped that his employers would be willing to negotiate; however, in this bureaucratic setting, each worker's role, salary, and working conditions were defined by uniform rules. The number of child cases assigned to a staff member was determined not by individual preference or even ability, but by a standard rule. A rule is formulated; it is then enforced by a superior. Such is the way of bureaucracy. When a high degree of bureaucratization limits the staff person's autonomy and control over his or her working conditions, job stress and burnout occur more frequently.

Although the benefits of greater staff autonomy and control in human service settings may seem obvious, some writers have questioned the wisdom of opening up the power structure of programs. For instance, Raskin (1973) argued that mental health workers may not want more responsibility in their jobs; in fact, they may *want* to be told what to do. Also, Raskin proposed that there are unusual organizational and administrative problems that make high levels of staff participation difficult to achieve as well as undesirable. However, Raskin offered no empirical evidence to support these beliefs, and the research on staff participation in decision-making in mental health programs cited by Cherniss and Egnatios (1978b) suggested (a) that staff definitely want a greater say in making decisions affecting their work, and (b) greater staff participation is associated with less role strain, more job satisfaction, better communication, and greater role clarity—all measures of organizational effectiveness. Thus, contrary to the earlier concerns and reservations offered by Raskin, greater staff participation in decision-making was not associated with greater organizational disruption and difficulty; in fact, greater participation seemed to have beneficial effects for the organization as well as the staff.

Thus, a program power structure characterized by centralized, hierarchical decision-making and a high degree of formalization limits the autonomy and control that staff members experience in their work. Such a power structure frustrates the staff person's quest for psychological success. Even when organizational imperatives are consistent with client welfare, the staff person increasingly feels like a small, easily replaceable cog in a large wheel. Burnout is an all-too-common consequence when autonomy and control are limited by the power structure of a human service.

THE NORMATIVE STRUCTURE AND BURNOUT

The goals, norms, and ideologies of human service programs represent the third major component of organizational design. They comprise the normative structure of the program. Although there is little systematic research on this aspect of the work setting, the research that has been done suggests that differences in the normative structures of programs affect the incidence of staff burnout.

Based on my previous discussion of role ambiguity as a major source of stress, one would expect that the strength and clarity of program goals would influence job stress. All programs have clearly stated goals that appear in grant proposals and public relations literature. Unfortunately, these goals tend to be general and vague. Also, there is little, if any, connection made between the general goals and the day-to-day operations of staff. Frequently, the staff are left on their own when it comes to developing and operationalizing a *guiding philosophy of treatment*. The guiding philosophy is not the same thing as the formal goals. The goals in an after-care program might be to restore normal functioning or to make the clients self-sufficient. An example of a guiding philosophy of treatment would be behavior modification. Programs in which the general goals are broken down into more specific operational objectives will tend to have lower levels of job stress. Also, programs in which there is a clear, distinctive guiding philosophy will tend to support higher involvement, hope, and commitment in staff (Reppuci, 1973; Colarelli & Siegel, 1966; Stotland & Kobler, 1965).

Many human service programs develop a guiding treatment philosophy; however the centrality and strength of the philosophy—the extent to which staff identify with it, understand it, and refer to it in performing their roles—vary considerably. For instance, many group homes for youth in which I have worked are based on the "token economy," "reality therapy," or "positive peer culture" philosophy. However, in many of these settings, the residential counselors tend to have little use for the "party-line." They tolerate it as a pet quirk of the administration or as something which is displayed for visitors as a way of enhancing their program's credibility. However, when it comes to working directly with the youth, the staff rely on their "intuition" or on an idiosyncratic treatment philosophy which is not necessarily shared or supported by co-workers and superiors. For instance, one staff person said: "The treatment model that we use here is the token economy. But I think that what really gets the kids to change is the development of a good, positive relationship with an adult figure." When asked how she tried to develop such a relationship with the youth, she never referred to the concepts or guiding principles of token economies or behavioristic psychology. She, and most of the other staff, saw the token economy as part of the bureaucratic structure to which they must conform. She did not use the program's guiding philosophy as a way of reducing uncertainty in her work with youth.

On the other hand, there have been a few group homes in which most staff enthusiastically supported and used the program's treatment philosophy. In these programs, the treatment philosophy was frequently referred to and used by staff in both formal meetings and informal discussions. They would engage in animated debates about what the guiding philosophy required in a particular case. They had so internalized the language and concepts of their treatment model that it would be difficult for an outsider to understand their case conferences unless he or she was familiar with the treatment philosophy. Interestingly, the guiding treatment philosophy in such programs did not seem rigid and fixed. The staff seemed to be engaged in constant elaboration and revision of the model, based on their clinical experience with it. In these programs, the staff appeared to be more involved and interested in their work and to experience less stress and frustration. Thus, a program treatment philosophy by itself does not seem to influence job stress and burnout. Only when that treatment philosophy "comes alive" for staff and becomes a central part of their thinking does it help sustain hope and involvement.

I am not suggesting that one treatment philosophy is better than another. Any of the dozens of theoretical approaches now prevalent in the human service field could serve as the unifying principle for a program. In fact, a unique conceptual framework developed by the staff themselves might be the most effective guiding philosophy. Neither am I suggesting that a program in which there is a strong, distinctive guiding philosophy is necessarily more effective in terms of hard measures of client outcome. I am merely proposing that when other things are equal, a distinctive, widely endorsed, and constantly used guiding treatment philosophy appears to reduce job stress and burnout in human service programs by increasing goal clarity and lowering role ambiguity.

Although greater goal clarity and a distinctive guiding philosophy can reduce job stress for staff, administrative attempts to impose greater goal clarity through "Management by Objectives" (MBO) or similar strategies frequently are resisted by staff because of the way these strategies are introduced. Too often, the staff are never involved in defining the role ambiguity problem or developing a solution. Thus, the administrative initiative is seen as a threat to staff autonomy and is resisted even though potentially it could be beneficial for staff.

Two examples of effective administrative efforts to reduce goal ambiguity and develop a distinctive guiding philosophy are presented in Colarelli and Siegel (1966) and Reppucci and Saunders (1975). The first work describes an innovative treatment program for chronic schizophrenics. Nonprofessional staff in this program initially had difficulty in assuming the role of therapist until the program directors involved the staff in a series of meetings for the purpose of developing a common framework for assessment and treatment. In the second example, the new superintendent of a juvenile correctional facility informed staff that changes were necessary; however, rather than imposing certain changes on the staff, he invited them to participate in discussion groups and task forces for the purpose of assessing the problems and developing proposals for dealing with them. Out of this process came a token economy plan which eventually became a core feature of the institution. In both of these examples, a guiding treatment philosophy for the program that was strongly endorsed by staff eventually emerged. The results may have been different if the same plans initially had been imposed on the staff by the administration. Thus, when it is sensitively developed and implemented, a strong and distinctive guiding treatment philosophy may reduce job stress and burnout. In general, there seems to be a relationship between the strength of the guiding philosophy and staff burnout in human service programs.

A second important aspect of the normative structure is *the strength of the bureaucratic mentality*. Job stress and burnout tend to be associated with the level of staff autonomy and control. The power structure affects autonomy and control in a direct way; greater centralization and formalization are associated with greater alienation, stress, and burnout. However, bureaucracy is a way of thinking as well as a formal mode of organization. Even though one program's power structure may allow as much formal autonomy and participation for staff as does another's, the "bureaucratic mentality" may be much stronger in the first program. Consequently, the staff in that program would *feel* less autonomous. Creativity and innovation are stifled not by the formal role and power structures, but by subtle norms that define the institutional atmosphere. The bureaucratic mentality—that is, an emphasis on avoiding risks, "covering" oneself, order, accountability, uniformity, and conformity—can suffuse the institutional culture, discouraging creativity, zest, and involvement in work even when formal autonomy is high. Thus, the extent to which innovation, creativity, and risk-taking are rewarded is an important aspect of a program's normative structure.[5]

The public schools represent a good example of how the bureaucratic mentality can limit individual initiative and freedom in staff even when formal role autonomy is high. The classroom teacher works virtually alone in the classroom and has a high degree of autonomy. However, the culture of the school encourages a high degree of conformity in the typical teacher (McIntyre, 1969; Sarason, 1971). For instance, McPherson (1972) recorded how older teachers nonverbally "reprimanded" new teachers whose classrooms became too noisy by closing their doors in a most definite and disapproving manner. The norm seemed to be that classrooms should be quiet and orderly, and any teacher who deviated from the norm was ostracized.

In an institution where the bureaucratic mentality is so strong, innovation and creativity are stifled. Consequently, the daily work of the staff loses much of its vitality over time. The job becomes less interesting and less fulfilling.

Although it is easy to criticize the typical public school for the bureaucratic mentality of its organizational climate, some settings in mental health are undoubtedly just as bureaucratic. Many state mental hospitals guarantee a high level of burnout for their staffs because of their bureaucratic climates. Within any human service field, one probably can find many programs in which the bureaucratic mentality is strong and growing stronger.

Unfortunately, we still do not know much about how the bureaucratic mentality develops. Bureaucratic structure—which contains a high degree of centralization and formalization—clearly is a strong contributing factor. However, the bureaucratic mentality can be strong even when the formal role and power structures are relatively nonbureaucratic. Some writers (for example, Sarason, 1972) have implied that the attitudes of organizational leaders, shaped by their interactions with an often hostile, threatening, or demanding external environment, are an important contributor to a bureaucratic mentality. Also, as organizations mature, the bureaucratic mentality seems to become stronger (Sarason, 1972). Whatever the causes, the degree to which a program encourages and rewards creativity, innovation, and nonconformity does seem to be related to the level of stimulation, interest, and involvement found in staff.

A third and related aspect of the normative structure that seems to be related to burnout is *the extent to which the production of new knowledge is an organizational goal.* Most human service programs are devoted entirely to service. Service to clients is seen as their sole concern; any other activity by staff is peripheral. However, some programs recognize the pursuit for knowledge as another legitimate goal and activity. It has been suggested that staff burnout occurs less frequently in programs that include research as an active concern. For instance, Mendel (1978: 19) wrote, "If the goal of a particular group is to develop better techniques, to write papers and books, to receive grants and professional recognition, then the provision of supportive care seems to cause much less staff burnout." In other words, research activity provides an alternative source of gratification for staff in a human service program. Staff who are encouraged to combine research with service in their jobs enjoy greater variety, autonomy, and intellectual stimulation than those who devote all of their time to direct service.

Of course, many human service workers have little interest in research, and it is not clear that introducing a research emphasis into their programs initially would be welcomed. However, this antipathy toward research in many cases may be based on misconceptions about the research process and a fear that research activity requires competencies which they lack. Many staff who now are hostile or indifferent to research might change their attitudes if they were able to participate in "action research"—research that helps one to better understand and more effectively handle the problems encountered in human service work (Price & Cherniss, 1976).

Some evidence concerning the benefits of a research focus for mental health programs comes from a study by Ellsworth et al. (1972). They examined "productivity" in the psychiatry wards of 39 VA hospitals. Productivity was measured by patient turnover and reduction of the long-term patient population. The most productive hospitals were contrasted with the least productive. The results indicated that in the most productive hospitals four times as many research studies were conducted. Although the researchers did not assess staff burnout, it seems likely that staff working in the most successful settings would feel more competent and efficacious and thus would experience less job stress and burnout. Thus, mental health programs that adopt the pursuit of knowledge as an important goal probably provide staff with more opportunities for stimulation and success. The extent to which the normative structure includes research as a goal also influences the rate of burnout.

The fourth and last way in which the normative structure of a program seems to impact on burnout is through *the norms concerning organizational health and staff needs*. Goldenberg (1971) observed that most human service programs are created with an implicit assumption that the psychological needs of staff are of relatively little importance. The focus is on the clients and their needs. Also, it is assumed that the organization's "health" will never be a major problem and that it therefore requires little ongoing attention. These implicit assumptions about the psychological needs and health of staff and organization become part of the program's normative structure; and it is likely that in programs where these needs are subordinated to others, burnout will be greater.

I once met a CMHC director who expressed this tendency to downplay the psychological needs of staff. He stated that the recent concern with staff burnout in the human services was merely a fad. He agreed that some staff members experience job stress, but he believed that few burn out. "Competent and mature professionals do not burn out," he stated. He believed that anyone who graduated from a recognized professional training program had been "inoculated" against burnout. In his eyes, the staff were—or at least should be—finished products. He said that staff who did burn out were obviously immature and neurotic, and they should not be working in the field. The main responsibility of the administrator was to identify those misfits and weed them out as soon as possible. Not surprisingly, there was considerable discontent among the staff in this setting.

Few administrators in the human service field are as hostile as this one was to the idea that staff experience stress in their work and need special support to help them cope with it. However, many do tend to regard job stress and burnout as relatively low-priority issues for the administration. In settings where this attitude permeates the normative structure, staff are likely to feel less support from the administration and co-workers. If their superiors regard them as easily replaceable machines, they may come to regard themselves in the same way. Also, if the institutional culture seems hostile or indifferent to their concerns, staff are likely to feel that they are powerless to change working conditions that contribute to stress. Change seems futile. A sense of helplessness increasingly pervades such settings, and the burnout rate is high.

When institutional norms discourage concern for the staff, organizational structures that could help staff cope with job stress are less likely to develop. For instance, it is unlikely that formal opportunities for staff to express and examine their feelings will be created; without such opportunities, staff are more likely to burn out (Maslach, 1976; Schwartz & Will, 1961).

Thus, the normative structure of a human service program influences job stress and burnout in at least four different ways: (1) the strength, clarity, and degree of staff identification with a guiding philosophy of treatment; (2) the strength and pervasiveness of the bureaucratic mentality; (3) the emphasis on learning, experimentation, and the production of knowledge as program goals; and (4) the degree of concern for staff and the work setting's impact on them. Staff respond directly to these aspects of the normative structure. Also, as Figure 5.1 suggests, the normative structure influences staff burnout indirectly through its impact on the role and power structures. For instance, a strong bureaucratic mentality is likely to lead to a more centralized, hierarchical, and formalized power structure. Less concern with staff and the job's impact on them is likely to lead to a role structure that generates high levels of role conflict and ambiguity. The normative structure of a program thus contributes to burnout in both direct and indirect ways.

Figure 5.1 summarizes what I suggested above about the organizational design's influence on job stress and burnout in human service programs. The three critical components of organizational design are the normative structure, the power structure, and the role structure. These components determine to a great extent the amount of role conflict and ambiguity experienced by any staff member. They also determine the extent to which any staff member's job is interesting, challenging, and stimulating. These three components also influence the amount of autonomy, participation, and control available to any staff member. All of these factors ultimately influence the extent to which staff members will experience "psychological success" in their work, which in turn will affect the burnout rate in the setting.

This model of organizational design and its impact on burnout is useful in three important ways. First, it provides a diagnostic framework with which program planners, administrators, and consultants can identify potential causes of job stress and burnout in a program. (See Cherniss, 1980b, for a step-by-step method for doing this.) Second, the model suggests specific areas for corrective intervention, as will be demonstrated more clearly in Chapter 9. Finally, the model suggests a number of interesting hypotheses to explore in future research. In fact, it should be emphasized that while the model is

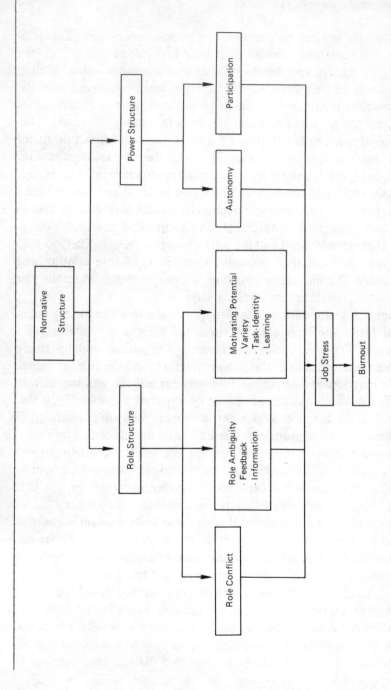

FIGURE 5.1   Impact of Organizational Design on Burnout

consistent with previous research, the amount and quality of that research leaves much to be desired. All of the propositions and relationships suggested by the model require further study and refinement. However, as a guide to research and practice, the model can be useful.

Notes

1. Support for this notion came from a study of community mental health programs which found that staff regard counseling or therapy with clients as more satisfying than mental health consultation or community organization. Staff also rated their self-confidence significantly higher for counseling and therapy than for consultation or other community work (Cherniss & Egnatios, 1978a).

2. In one study, 11 kinds of decisions affecting the working conditions of staff were identified: selection of supervisors, allocation of resources, hiring, promotions, pay increases, firings and layoffs, hours of work, work load, division of labor, work methods, and work quality standards (Cherniss & Egnatios, 1978b). Other decisions that have been studied include decisions regarding specific clients, planning of agency programs and procedures, and determining the order in which the day's work is performed (Sarata & Jeppesen, 1977). Obviously, for any particular program, this list of decisions could be greatly extended.

3. I recently consulted with a community mental health program that received funding from 17 different sources.

4. Some evidence for this notion came from the study of mental health programs by Cherniss and Egnatios (1978b) which found that higher levels of autonomy and participation in decision-making in a program were associated with less role ambiguity, more goal clarity, and better communication.

5. Although he did not discuss the concept of "bureaucratic mentality" as I have here, Moos (1974) developed measures and typologies of "social climate" that are relevant. A program characterized by a strong bureaucratic mentality would score high on Moos' measures of "order and organization" and "control."

Chapter 6

THE IMPACT OF SUPERVISION AND
SOCIAL SUPPORT FROM STAFF

Human service organizations are not mechanical, lifeless structures; they are composed of people. People work in them, and people manage them. The relationships among these people have a critical effect on job stress and burnout. The formal organizational design influences those social interactions; however, they also have their own impact independent of the organizational design. Of all the social interactions that influence job stress and the coping process in human service settings, the relationship between the supervisor and the worker is especially important.

LEADERSHIP AND SUPERVISION
AS A SOURCE OF BURNOUT

As I have noted elsewhere (Cherniss & Egnatios, 1978c) supervision in the human services is distinctive because it serves two different functions. First, like all forms of supervision, it is a major mechanism of administrative control. Supervisors monitor and evaluate the work of subordinates, ensuring a certain level of accountability and conformity to organizational rules. They also communicate important administrative decisions and directives which pass down the chain of command. Supervisors serve as important eyes and ears for the organization's leadership, keeping them informed about events, needs, and problems as they arise on the "firing line."

However, supervision in the human services also is intended to serve and support the worker in a way that would seem odd in a business or industrial setting. Supervision serves a "professional development" function as well as an administrative control function. All line staff, especially newer ones, look to their supervisors for support, advice, learning, and professional growth. At its best, supervision becomes a mentor relationship. There is a strong expectation that subordinates will learn and grow professionally as a result of their contact with their supervisors. In many settings, there also is a strong expectation that supervisors will help the worker to understand and constructively manage his or her own emotional response to the work. Thus, it should not be surprising that the quality of the supervisory relationship has a major impact on stress, strain and burnout in the job.

Previous research has amply documented the critical role of leadership and supervision in work groups. Conceptions of what constitutes "ideal" supervision have changed considerably over time, but the assumption that the quality of supervision is an important determinant of motivation and performance has remained intact. In the earliest formulations, the virtues of the "democratic" leader or supervisor were extolled (Lippitt & White, 1958). The ideal supervisor was warm, friendly, and considerate. He or she gave reasons for his or her actions and allowed the group to make many of the important decisions.

Later research and theory accepted this early formulation but added a second dimension: the effective leader also initiated and maintained task structure (Likert, 1961). High levels of motivation and performance required a supervisor who set high standards and helped the workers meet them. Through supervision, role conflict and ambiguity could be heightened or reduced.

Most recently, social and organizational psychologists increasingly have favored a "contingency" model of leadership, rejecting the original notion that there is a single ideal style of leadership and supervision. Fiedler (1967), a leading proponent of this school, conducted research suggesting that more democratic, human-relations-oriented leadership may not be as effective in certain kinds of situations.

Although the current status of research and theory on supervision is complex and confusing (there are still many prominent researchers who have not abandoned the older views and accepted the new contingency approach), the importance of supervision for morale and motivation remains unchallenged. One of the earliest studies documenting the critical role of supervision and leadership examined its influence in combat units during World War II. Grinker and Spiegel (1945) studied the factors contributing to job stress and "burnout" in one of the most hazardous types of work known (combat) and found that soldiers who were part of tight, cohesive groups coped better and worked more diligently. When Grinker and Spiegel searched for the factors that led to group cohesiveness, leadership emerged as the key variable.

Closer to home, research related to staff motivation in human service settings has confirmed the importance of supervision and leadership. For instance, a study of the priesthood found that the quality of the relationships between the priest and his pastor during the initial phase of the priest's career had a strong effect on his subsequent morale and commitment. The technical competence of the pastor also seemed to be important (Hall & Schneider, 1973). Pearlin (1967) found that the degree of alienation in hospital nurses was associated with the way in which their supervisor gave orders: Those supervisors who gave sensible reasons for their orders were less likely to have alienated subordinates than those who were more authoritarian and arbitrary.

Perhaps the most convincing research on the role of supervision in staff burnout was a study of 162 staff in 11 federally funded child abuse programs (Berkeley Planning Associates, 1977). Several factors in the work setting correlated with burnout, but a regression analysis indicated that leadership was the most important. Programs in which the leadership provided a high degree of structure and support tended to have lower levels of staff burnout.

Support and structure also characterized the supervision received by new professionals who were most resistent to burnout (Cherniss, 1980a). Those who showed the greatest amount of burnout during their first year of professional practice in a public human service agency generally worked under supervisors who were frequently unavailable and/or dictatorial and arbitrary.

The importance of supervision for what happens in the therapeutic process has long been recognized in the mental health field. For instance, an early study of psychiatric institutions suggested that disturbed interpersonal relations between a supervisor and a clinician are eventually reflected in disturbances in the therapeutic work between patient and therapist (Eckstein & Wallerstein, 1958). As the authors of this study put it, "The chain of supervision in the organization becomes a conduit for disturbances in interpersonal relations." Although this research did not assess the role of burnout in this process, the previously cited studies suggest that poor supervisory relationships may lead to more problematic therapeutic efforts, in part through their impact on job stress and coping in the clinician.

If supervision does influence job stress and burnout in human service programs, what qualities of supervisors are most important? Although the existing research is far from definitive, a tentative answer to this question is suggested. Generally, supervision that helps prevent burnout is characterized by a high degree of *support* which does not reduce the subordinate's *autonomy* (Hall & Schneider, 1973).

There are several kinds of support that staff seek from their supervisors. First, there is *technical assistance*. By suggesting better ways to handle difficult problems, a supervisor can increase a worker's efficacy and morale. Second, the supervisor can help the worker to *work through* the feelings generated by the helping process. As one mental health professional puts it, much of the strain and conflict generated by a particularly resistant client was alleviated when he discussed the case with his supervisor and she accepted his feelings. By being available and listening sympathetically, this supervisor helped prevent the development of burnout in this worker.

Supervisors also are supportive through the *information, modeling, and feedback* they provide to their subordinates. As we saw earlier, human service work is inherently ambiguous. However, supervisors can reduce the ambiguity by helping their staff to set reasonable priorities and goals for themselves. They also can serve as a point of reference for staff: for instance, a clinical social worker said that he felt more competent and secure when he and his supervisor saw a case the same way. Human service workers also look to their supervisors for the corrective feedback that often is not available from the work itself. Unfortunately, research in a variety of settings suggests that many supervisors tend to sidestep evaluation of their subordinate's work even though their subordinates state that they would welcome feedback—negative as well as positive—if it is given constructively (Kadushin, 1974; Lortie, 1973).

One other important way in which supervisors support their staffs is by acting as *buffers and advocates*. Human service workers often feel besieged by various community groups and bureaucratic agencies at the federal, state, and local level. They feel powerless before these larger forces. However, some of this powerlessness and the stress that accompanies it can be alleviated if the workers believe that their supervisors understand and support their interests and are able to effectively champion those interests in their dealings with other groups in the environment. A weak supervisor who appears to be an ineffective buffer and advocate for staff fails to provide them important support.

On the most basic level, though, supervisors help alleviate burnout by being responsive to the staff. One of the underlying causes of burnout is a sense of helplessness, a belief that one's responses have no effect on important sources of reinforcement. When supervisors are unresponsive, they unwittingly foster this condition. However, if supervisors are available, interested, and involved with their staff, then staff perceive a connection between what they do and an important source of reinforcement in the environment. Even negative feedback from supervisors can reduce a sense of helplessness if it is given constructively, consistently, and fairly. In fact, a supervisor who is always positive, no matter what the staff do, is as unresponsive to their actions as is the supervisor who is always negative. Responsiveness should lead staff to believe that they can influence an important source of reinforcement in the environment through their actions.

However, research on supervision suggests that staff need autonomy as well as support; the hovering, intrusive supervisor limits staff autonomy and control and thus may also contribute to frustration and stress. Even the supervisor who competently offers formulations and advice to staff during supervisory sessions may stifle their desire to work through problems on their own. Sometimes, staff want their supervisors to help them simply by asking questions, paraphrasing, and listening (Cherniss and Egnatios, 1978c). The staff want help, but they also want to retain a sense of ownership of their work. The following exerpt from an interview with a clinical social worker employed in a community mental health program suggests how easily a well-meaning, competent supervisor can infringe on a worker's autonomy:

> The other day I had an emergency, a client, a couple of clients, and I was feeling upset about things. But supervision means we get into stuff about clients very objectively and analyze it. And in a way, it feels like my supervisor's show, like she's doing a performance. The main thing that happens in supervision is she analyzes the client. And that's great for her. She really gets off on it. It can be exciting momentarily for me. And you know, she can help me see a little more clearly what's happening. But for me, that takes a lot of the fun out of it. My attitude is, "So you take that client then!" I don't want my supervisor to take it away from me, the joy of discovering how to work with this person.

In this example, the supervisor offered suggestions and interpretations which were helpful, but in doing so she reduced the worker's sense of autonomy and, consequently, he was deprived of the "joy of discovery." Also, the supervisor was task-oriented even when the worker would have preferred emotional support. The supervisor was not responsive to what the worker wanted. The supervisor's approach was uniform, and it was based more on her style and needs than on the worker's. Consequently, the worker felt that it was the supervisor's "show." A sense of helplessness and impotence developed in this worker in response to this supervision experience.

Research on attitudes toward supervision in human service staff has suggested that most would welcome direct advice and suggestions from their supervisors at times (Cherniss & Egnatios, 1978c). However, at other times they would prefer that their supervisors allow them to think through difficult problems on their own. And at still other times, they would like their supervisors to provide emotional support rather than specific advice; they want supervision to help them come to terms with their feelings and perceptions. However, most supervisors give direct suggestions, advice, and interpretations most of the time (Cherniss & Egnatios, 1978c). Like the supervisor described in the example above, they do not help workers to examine their own feelings or to think through cases on their own. Of course, the optimal style of supervision will vary with the worker and the situation. Again, the key is responsiveness: Effective supervisors are sensitive and responsive to the needs of their staff. Such responsiveness leads to the right combination of support and autonomy for each staff person.

However, it is all too easy to blame supervisors for poor or inadequate supervision. What are the factors that influence supervisory behavior? If supervision is a critical element in the development of burnout, then this question must be addressed.

Poor supervision may result in part from the supervisor's *attitudes or lack of skill*. Supervisors and administrators in the human services usually have had no training in supervision or personnel management. They have been trained as clinicians and promoted into their present positions without any additional training. Consequently, they are not prepared for the complexities of the role.

However, poor supervision also may be caused by *the nature of the supervisor's role*. Supervisors often are themselves the targets of enormous pressures, demands, and conflicts. They may be overwhelmed by demands to monitor paperwork and attend to other bureaucratic details. They may be constantly distracted by crises that require their attention. They may have too many workers to supervise. They may be troubled by the same kinds of professional-bureaucratic role conflicts that disturb their workers; in fact, the first-line supervisors in a human service organization usually are the ones who experience this conflict most intensely, for they are the people who mediate between the dominantly professional orientation of line staff and the bureaucratic orientation of higher-level administration

(Abrahamson, 1967). All of these pressures and conflicts could cause many supervisors to emotionally withdraw from their workers, to become less responsive to their needs, more authoritarian and arbitrary. In other words, supervisors in human service programs also may "burn out," and the quality of supervision will suffer when they do. Thus, supervision can be an important source of job stress and burnout in human service programs, and the quality of supervision is influenced by role pressures on the supervisor as well as the supervisor's attitudes, skill, and knowledge.

SOCIAL INTERACTION AND SUPPORT AMONG STAFF

All of the kinds of support that staff seek from supervisors also may be provided—or withheld—by their colleagues. First, discussing work problems with colleagues can be a cathartic experience that reduces emotional tension and helps the worker acquire better perspective and understanding. Second, colleagues are an invaluable source of technical information and practical advice. Third, colleagues provide a frame of reference and feedback by which the staff person may gauge the impact and quality of his or her work. Fourth, colleagues can provide a "united front" in conflicts with the organization or community groups. Finally, colleagues can be an important source of stimulation; when one can discuss work experiences with colleagues, those experiences often become more interesting and meaningful. Thus, in a number of ways, social interaction among colleagues in a program can help reduce job stress and burnout.

The benefits of social interaction and support in alleviating stress have been recognized for some time by researchers interested in stress generally and burnout in particular. For instance, Caplan et al. (1975) found that depression and somatic complaints were related to perceived low levels of social support from supervisors and others at work. Maslach (1976) observed that staff in human service agencies who are able to meet regularly with others in a "support group" are less likely to burn out. The group discussions help frustrated workers see that their problems and reactions are not unique. This in itself seems to reduce the emotional strain. However, ideas exchanged among members of these support groups also may suggest concrete ways of coping with the demands that contribute to the strain.

Although social interaction often provides support for those facing stress in their lives, it sometimes has the opposite effect. For instance, in a study of graduate students preparing for their qualifying exams, Mechanic (1962) found that greater interaction with peers led to heightened stress in many instances. Students who were most isolated during this period tended to experience the lowest levels of stress and difficulty. The same phenomenon has been reported to me by staff in human service programs who have participated in group discussions concerned with work-related problems: In some instances these discussions have degenerated into "bitch sessions" which only made people feel worse and led to no improvement in the situation. Thus, social interaction with colleagues may provide support and alleviate stress for human service workers, but this positive outcome is by no means certain. Nevertheless, the *potential* benefits of social interaction for frustrated staff are great, and the professional isolation that sometimes occurs in programs itself can be a source of stress and strain.

Unfortunately, many systemic factors contribute to professional isolation in human service settings. Mistrust, conflict, and hostility among individuals and groups within a program represent one major barrier to social interaction and support. There are several potential sources of conflict and mistrust; one of the most common is *differences in values and theoretical orientation*. For instance, in one mental health program that I studied, the staff seemed to be split into two major groups: those who favored the psychoanalytic approach and those who followed Transactional Analysis. According to a new staff person, those associated with one group had little interest in or even tolerance for those who supported the other. A climate of mistrust in which there was little discussion of work-related ideas and concerns prevailed as a result of this split among the staff.

In other cases, the conflict is caused by *differences in personal values*. In one study (Cherniss, 1980a), I found that newer, more idealistic professionals in a human service agency often avoided contact with more experienced staff whom they perceived to be cynical and lacking in dedication. An example was a clinical social worker who refused to go to picnics and parties with co-workers because he did not want to be "exposed" to the negative attitudes he associated with "professionalism." Thus, perceived differences in personal values and treatment philosophy can impede the development of social support among staff in human service settings.

Differences in and competition over scarce resources, status, and power also can create a climate of mistrust and social isolation in a program. Any perceived difference in privileges can lead to bitterness and conflict in a social system, and differences are inevitable in large, formal organizations. For instance, in one setting, the director typically ate lunch with one staff group rather than the others, and his relations with the first group were warmer and closer. This situation was fine for the staff in this group, but staff in the other groups resented the "favored" ones. They became bitter because they were denied a privilege given to others. The director's apparent favoritism created an atmosphere of envy and rivalry rather than support.

Role conflict and ambiguity also can drive a wedge between staff in a setting. Kahn et al. (1964) found that withdrawal from social interaction with role senders was a typical response to role conflict and ambiguity in organizational settings. In the previous chapter, I described the problem encountered by social worker Diane Peterson who was employed by one agency but assigned to work part-time in another. There was some confusion about when she would start working at the second agency, and staff at that second agency thought she would begin sooner than she did. Also, when she finally did arrive on the scene, the other staff expected that she would share intake and other regular staff responsibilities; but her boss expected that she would avoid such work and instead serve as a "consultant" and trainer for the other staff. Even after the confusion and conflict were cleared up, Diane's relationships with other staff members were strained. Unfortunately, these kinds of misunderstandings occur frequently in the complex organizational arrangements that characterize many human service programs.

Even when a program's role structure does not create high levels of conflict and ambiguity, it can be a barrier to positive social interaction and support among staff. *Heavy work loads* are an example. One new worker whom I interviewed said that her efforts to obtain information and advice from her colleagues often were thwarted because everyone was so busy just trying to keep up. Because the staff felt that they barely had enough time for their clients, they had even less time for one another. The message seemed to be, "We don't have time to help, so just stay out of our way."

In other cases, *the structure of work limits opportunities for staff interaction.* For instance, staff in many mental health settings are alone with clients much of the day. They have open hours and brief periods between appointments when they can interact with co-workers. Certainly, compared with public school teachers who are confined to a classroom most of the day, mental health workers are less isolated from colleagues. However, compared with those in many other occupations, mental health workers have more limited opportunity for relaxed, informal interaction with co-workers.

As workers in human service programs spend increasing amounts of time in community work, isolation from co-workers is likely to become even greater. Their plight will come to resemble the public health nurse's, one of whom said:

> You go from family to family or school to school, and you really aren't working with people as you are in an office. And you get kind of lonely, sometimes, or you want to talk about something because you're listening to all these problems people have, and just venting a few of your own feelings sometimes is really important. . . . It's nice to be able to communicate with people you work with, especially if there's a problem. But you're not in the office that much. You come here to do paperwork or make phone calls, and then you just leave and get on your way [Cherniss, 1980a].

Informal norms of social interaction in a setting can be as formidable a barrier as the formal role structure. Even when human service workers can overcome the barriers of differences in treatment philosophy and values, role conflict and ambiguity, and rivalry over status and resources, social support may be impeded by certain patterns of social interaction. For instance, in many settings the serious discussion of work-related issues seems to be taboo in informal settings such as the lunch room. A common style of interaction around the coffee pot or in the lunch room is light, jovial, sarcastic bantering that jumps quickly from one topic to another. Although this kind of interaction probably provides a welcome and needed escape for emotionally strained workers, it can interfere with the development of social support for work-related problems.

The weekly staff meeting is another setting in which there may be patterns of interaction that stifle social support. Too often, these meetings become dominated by one-way perfunctory communication of administrative information. Genuine interchanges of ideas, open and creative discussion of work-related concerns, and mutual support would seem to be foreign and out-of-place in such settings. As one dissatisfied worker in a community program put it, "I don't like to sit in a meeting and have someone tell me what we're going to do for the week, and then get up and leave. We have meetings that last five minutes, and it's ridiculous." She felt cheated because she believed that many of her colleagues had much to offer, and the pattern of interaction at staff meetings prevented them from sharing it.

Even when staff meetings allow discussion of work-related concerns, the dominant style of interaction may limit the amount of real sharing and support that occurs. One mental health worker described case conferences in his program in the following way:

> Case presentations are pretty much a drag. . . . One person will say something, and someone will respond, and it won't be directly to what the first person said. And then, the presenter is "lost" in the process. Another mode is, you present, and then everyone just tells you what to do. And even though we had this big rap that people wouldn't do that unless the person asked for it, they're doing it anyway. We didn't change anything. So I haven't felt it yet, like the real excitement of sharing in a staff meeting, and no one else has ever reported feeling that way either.

As this quote suggests, norms of social interaction can interfere with the development of social and intellectual support among co-workers even when such support is an explicit purpose of the interaction. This quote also suggests how strongly entrenched and difficult to change these patterns of interaction can be.

Thus, social interaction among colleagues in human service programs represents a potentially important source of support for adaptive coping with work-related stress, but there often are numerous barriers to the development of supportive interaction in these settings. Differences in treatment ideology, personal values, status, resources, and power can easily lead to mistrust, competition, and conflict. Role conflict, ambiguity, and overload also can interfere with social support. The role structure also can severely limit opportunities for social interaction and support. Finally, informal norms of social interaction may interfere with support even when other factors are favorable.

CONCLUSION: BURNOUT, THE WORK PLACE, AND THE EXTERNAL ENVIRONMENT

Factors contributing to job stress and burnout in human service programs can be found at three different levels of analysis: the individual, the work setting, and the larger culture and society. Although all three levels are important, the work setting offers the most promise for effective intervention.

The three primary sources of burnout in the work setting are the organizational design, leadership and supervision, and social interaction among staff. These factors are interrelated in important ways. For instance, supervisors and administrators have some control over a program's organizational design. We have already seen that the role structure influences social interaction and support among staff. The institutional norms and other aspects of organizational design influence what kinds of people become supervisors and administrators. Many other interactions between the various factors could be identified as well.

An important topic I have ignored is the influence of the external environment on the work setting. The nature of the community served by the program probably has a strong impact on those aspects of the work setting that influence burnout. For instance, the kind of stress experienced by staff probably differs in rural and urban programs. Local politics and attitudes, shaped by a community's social and economic history, will influence the level of funding and support given to a program, which may, in turn, affect burnout rates. Even physical characteristics of a community such as climate and topography may influence job stress and burnout in programs.

The relationships between the program and other community organizations also should influence staff burnout. For instance, in a

community where the social service and mental health agencies traditionally have competed and remained aloof from one another, the
burdens and obstacles for mental health staff probably will be greater
than in communities where the different agencies have shared information more freely and cooperated. The work climate of a program
also will be influenced by regional, state, and federal agencies that
play a role in mental health policy and programs. I have already
referred to the Sarata and Reppucci (1974) study which suggested that
decisions made by state and federal authorities can increase job stress
and interpersonal conflict in a program when those decisions threaten
the program's integrity. Thus, the human service program's external
environment will influence job stress and organizational burnout in
numerous ways. Unfortunately, this important source of burnout has
been almost totally neglected in previous research and writing on this
topic. It is hoped that future work in this area will fill this gap in our
knowledge.

Chapter 7

INDIVIDUAL FACTORS IN JOB STRESS

Any job that is high in role conflict and ambiguity, low in autonomy and variety, and situated in an organization that provides poor supervision will generate much job stress and burnout in its occupants. However, people differ in their vulnerability to stress and in their coping effectiveness. An analysis of burnout would be incomplete if these individual factors were not considered. Research on stress and coping suggests that certain personality traits, career goals, and previous experience may influence one's susceptibility. The amount of social support and stress experienced by the individual outside of work also plays a role.

PERSONALITY TRAITS, STRESS, AND COPING

Five personality traits have been found to influence an individual's response to stress: neurotic anxiety, the "Type A" syndrome, locus of control, flexibility, and introversion. *Neurotic anxiety* actually is a constellation of traits and dispositions that tend to occur together. One of the most important is excessive and conflicting motivation.

Neurotically anxious individuals have strong, punitive superegos. They set extremely high goals for themselves and punish themselves severely if they fail to achieve those goals. They also suffer because their goals and aspirations conflict with one another, and they are unable to resolve those conflicts. So, for instance, a strong desire for success will conflict with an equally strong fear of competition and need for approval. In the neurotically anxious individual, any strong motivation—whether it be achievement aspiration, dependency need, power and status need, or sex drive—is in a perpetual state of conflict with strong moral prohibitions.

A second trait associated with neurotic anxiety is emotionality and instability. The neurotically anxious individual is more emotional than others, and this emotionality often interferes with adaptive functioning. In the face of conflict and stress, the person is easily overcome by powerful anxiety. The person tends to be fearful and apprehensive in any new situation. Anger, depression, and other emotions also may be pronounced. Inadequate coping tendencies represent a third characteristic of neurotic anxiety. The neurotically anxious individual tends to act impulsively, lacks perseverence, and relies heavily on defense mechanisms such as denial, repression, and projection. The final feature of neurotic anxiety is low self-esteem and an excessive concern with the opinion of others. The neurotic tends to emphasize and dwell upon his or her weaknesses and deficits. There is a strong need to be accepted and liked by others. Thus, the individual who is high in neurotic anxiety will display strong and conflicting motivations, high emotionality, low self-esteem, an excessive concern with the approval of others, and a reliance on defense mechanisms as a means of coping.

Kahn et al. (1964) found that individuals who scored high in neurotic anxiety (as measured by a pencil-and-paper test) experienced more strain and tension in high role conflict situations than did those who scored low on this trait. They also found that neurotics were less likely to withdraw from others in high role conflict situations, probably because of their strong dependency needs. Interestingly, this tendency to rely on others in the face of role conflict probably helped them to cope more effectively with the conflict than did those who withdrew, for withdrawal tends to exacerbate role conflict and ambiguity in organizations.

In one of the earliest studies of reaction to stress, Grinker and Spiegel (1945) found that unrealistic, neurotic motivation was a major cause of negative stress reactions in combat fliers. In one of the first papers to refer to burnout in the human services, Freudenberger (1975) suggested that the "dedicated and committed" are the most prone to burnout. He also proposed that those with a strong need to be accepted and liked were at risk. Similarly, Pines and Kafry (1978) found that mental health professionals who were lower in self-esteem tended to be more dissatisfied with their work and rated their job performance lower than others. Finally, Lazarus and Launier (1978) suggested that an individual's sense of vulnerability and susceptibility to stress are increased by a belief that a setting is hostile or dangerous and by feelings of inadequacy.

Unfortunately, the human services may attract individuals who have strong dependency and achievement needs, set unrealistically high standards for themselves, and display other traits associated with neurotic anxiety. They are people who want to "rescue" others and who feel miserable when they fail. They are achievers who have performed well in advanced educational programs. They seek to provide emotional support to others because that kind of emotional support is so important to them. Of course, this description is almost a caricature. The personality structures of mental health workers vary so much that generalizations would be difficult to make. However, there is no doubt that the dispositions associated with neurotic anxiety can be found to a greater or lesser degree in many who work in the field, and these factors will make one more susceptible to stress.

Another individual characteristic that makes one more susceptible to stress, especially in a work situation, is the *"Type A" personality*. According to Friedman and Rosenman (1974), certain individuals seem prone to a striving, competitive, time-pressured lifestyle, while others are characteristically more calm and relaxed in their approach to life. These authors identified the driven, pressured style as Type A personality; they have produced research suggesting that Type A individuals experience more stress-related illness, especially coronary heart disease. Friedman and Rosenman (1974: 4) describe the Type A syndrome as a particular complex of traits, including excessive competitive drive, aggressiveness, impatience, and a harrying sense of time urgency. Individuals displaying this pattern seem to be engaged in a chronic, ceaseless, and often fruitless struggle—with themselves, with others, with circumstances, with time, and sometimes with life itself.

The Type A syndrome is regarded as a coping style or deeply ingrained personality trait. Although no one has published research on the link between the Type A personality and burnout, the link between stress and burnout suggests that Type A individuals may be more likely to burn out than others.

Unfortunately, there is reason to believe that many workers in human service programs—particularly professionals—are likely to be Type A personalities. Several studies have suggested that physicians, dentists, psychologists, and other helping professionals are more prone to Type A than those in other fields (Howard et al, 1976; Russek & Russek, 1976; Friedman, 1978). This finding should not be surprising, for successful completion of the long and arduous schooling necessary for professional credentials requires precisely those traits associated with the Type A syndrome. The structure of the human services and of the larger society ensures that a large proportion of those selected to work in human service programs will be Type A individuals who may well be prone to burnout.

Locus of control is a third personality dimension that has been linked to differences in stress reactions. According to Rotter (1966), individuals differ in the degree to which they believe that they control important sources of reinforcement in their lives. "Internals" tend to believe that they control their destinies. If they want something, they assume they can get it. If they fail, it is because they lacked the will or the ability. "Externals" believe they are at the mercy of fate or powers beyond their control. Whether life turns out well or poorly for them, they attribute the cause not to their own efforts or abilities but to external forces.

Seligman (1975) suggested that "externals" are more prone to learned helplessness. In other words, they are more likely to believe that they are helpless and have no control over a situation and, consequently, will tend to give up and withdraw in the face of stress and frustration. Internals, on the other hand, will tend to persist in the face of frustration. They are less likely to manifest the motivational deficits associated with learned helplessness and burnout.

Flexibility is another personality trait that affects reactions to stress. Although those who work in the human services may value flexibility and condemn rigidity (for many good reasons), evidence suggests that the flexible individual may be more susceptible to stress, especially in a helping occupation. Kahn et al. (1964) found that flexibile individuals were more likely to experience role conflict in work organizations, and they reacted to role conflict with more manifest anxiety, tension, and worry than did rigid individuals. Flexible persons seemed to be more susceptible to role conflict, in part because they found it more difficult to say "no" to role senders who came to them with extra demands.

However, rigid individuals were not immune from role conflict and stress, and they did not cope nearly as well as their more flexible co-workers when stress occurred. The rigid were more likely to reject role senders and withdraw socially. They also were more likely to develop a sense of futility (which is the core of the burnout syndrome) and to become more dependent on authority figures, more compulsive in their work habits, and more prone to use denial and projection. Thus, while flexibility may make a person more susceptible to stress, it also may contribute to more adaptive coping when stress occurs.

One final personality trait associated with stress reactions is *introversion*. Kahn et al. (1964) found that introverts experienced more tension in high role conflict situations than did extroverts. Also, as one would expect, introverts were more likely to withdraw from their co-workers in the face of conflict and stress, and this withdrawal impeded effective coping and resolution of the conflict.

Thus, at least five personality traits have been found to be associated with reactions to stress. Neurotic anxiety, locus of control, flexibility, the Type A syndrome, and introversion seem to influence both the amount of tension and strain experienced by the individual and the way in which the individual typically copes. However, the influence of these personality traits should not be overestimated. The structure of the job and work organization ultimately is a stronger determinant of the incidence of burnout than is the individual's personality makeup.

CAREER-RELATED GOALS AND ATTITUDES

Perhaps even more important than personality traits in an individual's response to job stress are career-related goals, values, and attitudes. Every individual creates a number of goals which define what will be rewarding in the job. Although most individuals working in a particular occupation will share certain goals (for example, good salary, interesting work, pleasant co-workers), they will differ to some extent in their priorities. Also, some goals may be pursued only by certain workers and not others. Individuals also differ in their philosophy and approach. For instance, in mental health programs, some workers will value long-term treatment with troubled individuals more than consultation and education in the community. Consequently, they will react differently to performing these activities. Job stress would increase if these individuals were forced to engage in consultation and education work. On the other hand, other workers might prefer to do consultation and education and might find long-term treatment work a strain.

Two sets of attitudes toward work that have received much attention in previous research are the *professional and bureaucratic role orientations*. As noted in Chapter 5, much role conflict can occur when professionally oriented individuals work in bureaucratically organized institutions. The professional orientation emphasizes the uniqueness of both the client and the professional. Autonomy and collegial authority are emphasized. The bureaucratic orientation emphasizes efficiency, standardization, and subservience to a central organizational authority.

In helping occupations such as mental health, many individuals will come to their work with a strong professional orientation. However, there will be some who identify more strongly with the values of the bureaucratic orientation. Their supervisors will tend to reinforce those bureaucratic values, and there is evidence that over time, the bureaucratic orientation in nurses, social workers, and other groups tends to increase (Kramer, 1974). In fact, one can use these two orientations to define four separate "role configurations" based on whether an individual is high or low on each dimension. Thus, there will be some individuals working in a human service program who are high on the professional orientation and low on the bureaucratic.

Others will be high-bureaucratic and low-professional. Still others may be low on both dimensions: These would be individuals who remain somewhat disengaged from the kinds of conflicts generated by professional versus bureaucratic standards and who easily follow whatever orientation is easiest at any given point in time. In other words, the ideological issues involved are not particularly important to them. A final group may be high on both dimensions, recognizing the legitimacy and value of both orientations and trying to develop an approach to work that remains consistent with both.

Kramer (1974) and Corwin (1961) studied individual differences in bureaucratic and professional role orientation and their impact on stress and satisfaction. Both researchers found that conflict and stress potentially were highest for those who were simultaneously high in bureaucratic and professional values. (Kramer's work suggested that these individuals also were potentially the most effective.) The group that experienced the next greatest conflict was the high-professional, low-bureaucratic group. Although Kramer believed that individuals could be taught to cope with the stress and conflict inherent in identifying strongly with both orientations, there seems little doubt that individuals who have this particular role configuration will experience more job stress in human service programs than will those who are primarily bureaucratic in orientation or weak in both.

A somewhat related role orientation is *social activism*. Most workers in a helping occupation will be concerned primarily with providing service to individuals. They wish simply to help individuals; they are not interested in using the job to effect change in their profession, the community, or the larger society. They may become involved in political efforts to change society, but they do so outside of work and keep the two roles of "professional" and "citizen" separate.

However, another group of individuals sees its work as a vehicle for bringing about institutional change. For instance, one individual I interviewed was concered about the inequities in the delivery of mental health services to white and nonwhite populations. One of her goals in entering the mental health field was to work toward changing the system in a way that would reduce those inequities. Another individual worked in the schools as a mental health consultant and sought to use that role to change what he saw as an extremely oppressive, "totalitarian" system. These professionals who seek to bring about social and institutional change through their work are the "social activists"; and there is some evidence that these individuals experience more job stress than others (Cherniss, 1980a; Wilensky, 1956).

Another individual trait that may influence burnout is *achievement motivation*. Some individuals will be more achievement-oriented than others, and there is evidence suggesting that the relative importance of achievement and success as opposed to security as career motives will affect the level of stress and style of coping. For instance, Kahn et al. (1964) identified three groups of workers based on their attitudes concerning achievement and security. For the "expertise-achievement-oriented" group, satisfaction came primarily from doing their work well. Extrinsic rewards were less important. They sought work situations that would allow them to successfully accomplish challenging tasks and utilize valued skills. They also were eager to develop and improve those skills and to acquire new ones that would enable them to perform even more effectively.

A second group studied by Kahn et al, the "status-achievement-oriented," consisted of individuals motivated primarily by a desire for career advancement. These "careerists" wanted to achieve recognition from their peers and superiors and rise in the organization or profession. They sought status, power, respect, financial rewards, and all of the other benefits commonly associated with success as it is traditionally defined. The final group eschewed achievement and success; for them, security was the most important reward. They were less ambitious and less involved in their work than those in the other two groups. Their internal standards for performance were relatively modest, and they were not particularly perturbed if they were passed over for promotion. They avoided situations that threatened their job security, even if those situations offered the possibility for future advancement and success.

After identifying these three motivational dispositions, Kahn et al. (1964) studied their reactions to the stress of high role conflict in a work organization. The findings showed that the status-oriented careerists experienced more tension in response to high role conflict, probably because they were more involved in the job and attributed high importance to it relative to other areas of their lives. Also, the career advancement they sought depended on their fulfillment of the role demands made by co-workers and superiors; thus, a situation in which there were seemingly irreconcilable conflicts in those demands was particularly threatening. On the other hand, the expertise-oriented workers also were highly involved in their work, but their work-related goals were less affected by the opinions of others. Consequently, they, like the security-oriented group, were less affected by high role conflict.

However, the expertise-oriented individuals tended to cope with high role conflict in ways that were probably less adaptive in the long run. Kahn et al. found that those in this group were more likely to withdraw from others, especially important role senders, in the face of high role conflict. In withdrawing, they made it more difficult to resolve the source of the conflict, and they contributed to a situation which might lead to more role conflict and ambiguity in the future. Security-oriented and success-oriented workers were less likely to withdraw from important role senders when confronted with high role conflict. Thus, the relative strength of achievement, success, and security as job-related motives seems to influence both the amount of stress experienced in the job and the ways in which individuals cope with it. It should be recognized, however, that Kahn et al. examined the effects of one type of stress: role conflict. Other types of job stress, such as lack of variety or task identity in the work, or lackadaisical, unsupportive supervision, might have very different effects. While individual differences in values and motives clearly influence the response to stress, the structure of the work situation remains an important factor.

THE IMPACT OF PREVIOUS EXPERIENCE

In a sense, everything I have discussed in this chapter is related to previous experience; personality traits, role orientations, and career-related goals and motives all are the products of past experience. However, more specific connections between previous experience and reactions to job-related stress can be made.

Perhaps the most obvious generalization is that prior experience with the task, the stressor, and/or the situation attenuates the effects of stress (McGrath, 1970). For instance, an individual who has done mental health consultation in the past probably will experience less stress than one who has never engaged in this activity before. Similarly, those who have had to deal with a particular type of role conflict in the past should be less perturbed when it arises in a new situation. Of course, if they have not coped effectively with that role conflict in the past and it has led to perceived harm, they may become more disorganized by it than someone who has never had any such experience. Mechanic (1962) found that graduate students who had failed their qualifying exams in the past were more anxious before taking them again than were their peers who had never taken them before.

This last consideration suggests that the extent to which one has gained mastery in the past may be especially important in determining how one copes with stress in the present and future. Long ago, Lewin (cited in Hall, 1976) recognized that individuals who experience "psychological success" in a role emerge with greater self-esteem, optimism, and involvement. They are ready to accept new challenges and are less likely to suffer incapacitating stress when the challenges become difficult. More recently, Seligman (1975) argued that past experiences of mastery "inoculate" people against learned helplessness and depression. For instance, in one experimental study Seligman exposed two groups of animals to the basic learned helplessness situation. One group had been carefully raised in the laboratory from birth so that they experienced no traumas, no discomforts—and thus no mastery over challenge. The second group consisted of animals that had grown up "on the streets" and who presumably had been forced to deal with and overcome numerous difficulties. The results showed that the laboratory-raised animals were more likely to give up when confronted with stress from which they could not immediately escape. The animals who had a legacy of mastery tended to persist in their efforts to overcome the challenge. Thus, mastery gained in the past seems to increase the attitudinal and motivational factors that make one less vulnerable to stress and more capable of coping with it effectively.

However, the kind of situation in which mastery was achieved, and its relevance to current challenges, probably is important. For instance, those who have reached higher levels of educational attainment undoubtedly have had to master many challenges and stresses. This might lead one to expect that higher educational levels would be associated with less job stress and burnout. However, the research suggests a very different picture. In fact, two different studies found that service providers with post-baccalaureate training were more likely to experience burnout than were providers with less education (Berkeley Planning Associates, 1977; Maslach and Jackson, 1978).

Age and sex are two other personal characteristics found to be associated with burnout in the human services. Maslach and Jackson (1978) found that younger workers scored higher on two measures of burnout than did older workers. The pattern for sex was more complicated: Females scored higher in "emotional exhaustion" and lower on "personal accomplishment," two dimensions of burnout measured by the Maslach Burnout Inventory; however, males scored higher on "depersonalization," a third dimension used in the scale. This suggests that male and female workers in human service fields may not differ in the amount of stress experienced in the job but do cope with it differently. Thus, previous experience, educational history, age, and sex are personal factors that seem to influence vulnerability to job stress and the way in which one copes with it.

IS THERE LIFE AFTER WORK?

Previous research on job stress and coping has tended to focus exclusively on the work setting, ignoring factors in the individual's life outside work that could influence one's reaction to work-related stress. Fortunately, more recent research is expanding the scope of inquiry and correcting this bias in our conception of the work experience (Kane, 1977; Piotrkowski, 1979; Cherniss, 1980a; Perlman & Hartman, 1979). Not surprisingly, we are finding that the quality of life outside work strongly influences one's reaction to a job.

One's personal life influences adaptation to the job in at least two ways. First, friends and relatives represent a potentially important source of support. In fact, they can provide many of the same kinds of social support that colleagues provide (Chapter 6). However, these personal relationships outside work also can impose demands and obligations; thus, they create the possibility of role conflict that can add to strain in the job.

An example of how people outside work can help one to cope with the strains of the job was provided by a clinical social worker interviewed as part of a study of burnout in new professionals (Cherniss, 1980a). Hers was a particularly demanding and frustrating job, and she said that she relied heavily on the acceptance and support she received from the person she was dating and from her many friends. After a hard day at work, she could go home and talk to these people. They would respond with sympathy, acceptance, helpful comments, questions, and suggestions. After a short while, she would feel much better about the problems at work. Her emotional exhaustion would dissipate, and she could face the prospect of returning the next day. These personal ties were important to this mental health professional, an "important source of energy" in her life. As she put it, "I have to feel good about myself, and there's only so much of that I can do myself."

An interesting research finding concerning the relationship between marital status and burnout tends to support the notion that close, personal relationships outside work help to mitigate the strains associated with the job. Maslach and Jackson (1978) found that human service workers who were single or divorced reported feeling more emotional exhaustion from their work than did married individuals. Of course, one cannot say with certainty that being married helped reduce stress in the job. It could be, for instance, that married individuals tend to choose less demanding jobs. However, the personal comments of helping professionals suggest that close, supportive personal relationships do alleviate the strain of work (Cherniss, 1980a).[1]

Participation in activities outside work also can be a source of emotional support and an important alternative source of gratification. For instance, one mental health worker I interviewed had become involved in a personal awareness and growth program at a local training center. The program took an additional ten hours of his time each week, but it was the major source of gratification and fulfillment in his life. The problems associated with his job seemed less distressing because he always could look forward to this other experience. Another new professional became involved in karate shortly after beginning her career. This activity served as an alternative means of achieving a sense of efficacy and psychological success. Not only did the physical activity help to siphon off tension, but the improvement in skill and strength, signified by progress from one color belt to another, provided her with the rewards that were so often missing in her job. Thus, outside activities and commitments can be alternative sources of social support and fulfillment that help one to better cope with the psychological strains of a demanding job.

Unfortunately, activities and relationships outside work can create strain in the human service worker as well as alleviate it. Work-family role conflict is a common problem in our society, and when it is severe, it can seriously impede an individual's adaptation to a job. In work-family role conflict, the obligations and demands associated with the work role come into conflict with those associated with family roles ("family" can be defined broadly to include nonfamilial loved ones as well as spouses, children, and other relatives). A particularly good description of this problem was provided by a new mental health professional. In the following passage, he describes how the demands of his job made him less emotionally and physically available to his wife, and he notes that this created additional strain for both of them:

> My job pretty much defines home life. It cuts down the number of hours I have. I'm home less than I was when I was still a student. Towards the beginning of my employment, when I came home, I did not want to talk. I especially did not want to talk shop. I just wanted to be left alone. I hoped that my wife wouldn't ask me about work, but she usually did. She's a social work student, and she just had an interest. She became frustrated at times. She took it personally. But the more she got into her field placement, the more she understood how I felt.

> I think we've both been kind of lackadaisical about the house, too, which is also a problem. We both like to spend time cooking and taking care of the house, but since for me the time off is limited, it

makes it difficult to stay on top of everything. From time to time it's caused pressures on our relationship. Sometimes we really want this place to look as neat as it's ever looked. We get really frustrated because then we have to go on a whirlwind binge to clean the place up. One problem is when one of us wanted to work and the other didn't. Sunday mornings I want to become a puddle and she wants to clean.

Fortunately, this particular couple seemed to be adapting relatively well to the problems of work-family role conflict; however, even in their case, it is easy to see how the demands of the job led to conflict and the need for accommodation in family relationships.

This last quote also suggests that differences in family factors may influence stress and the coping process. In a study cited earlier, Mechanic (1962) found that the family's response to a member's stress was strongly influenced by the nature of family relationships and commitments prior to the onset of the stress. Stress outside the family required a change in family role expectations and behavior. Couples with no children seemed better able to make those accommodations than others. Also, when both spouses were students, or when one had a relatively satisfying and nonstressful job of his or her own, the family and the individual adapted better to stress. Thus, in the case described above, the strains might have been even greater if the spouse had not been a student in a similar field or if the couple had had children.

Further evidence for the potential conflict between work and family life came from a study of burnout in police officers by Maslach and Jackson (1978). They found that officers scoring high on a measure of burnout were more likely to want to be alone when they were at home and more likely to get angry with their spouses. Thus, the stresses and strains encountered in a demanding human service job "spill over" and affect the family (Piotrkowski, 1979). The family's response affects how well the individual is able to cope with those stresses, and human service workers clearly will vary in the relative degree of conflict and support experienced in their families. Like personality traits, career goals, and previous experience, the quality of one's life outside of the job will influence one's vulnerability to stress and one's ability to cope with the stress that occurs.

Note

1. How much spouses and friends help alleviate job-related strain will depend in part on their behavior. For instance, Mechanic (1962) found that graduate students adapted better to stress when their spouses accepted the student's definition of the situation. More "objective," less supportive spouses were less helpful.

Chapter 8

HISTORICAL AND CULTURAL
SOURCES OF BURNOUT

Human service programs and staff do not exist in a social or historical vacuum; there is a larger context that greatly affects day-to-day functioning. Various social and institutional forces operating at the level of the larger society greatly influence both the individual and the program. Some of these larger forces are all too apparent, but others become evident only by studying our social history. In fact, a consideration of this society's recent past suggests why the topic of burnout has become so "relevant" today. Apparently, it is no coincidence that in the last five years the topic has burst upon the scene with much fanfare and interest. Burnout probably has always been a problem in the human services, but various changes in the social and political climate of the country have made people more aware of the problem now and more insistent about doing something to rectify it. By studying these historical roots of our current interest in burnout, we can learn much about how the institutional context influences job stress and burnout in human service programs.

THE DECLINE OF COMMUNITY

At one time, many of the human services now provided by formal organizations were provided instead by informal community groups and structures. To a much greater extent communities took care of themselves. This was especially true of mental health services. Until this century, only the most seriously disturbed individuals came into contact with a mental health setting. Many of the less disabling psychological and interpersonal problems were not defined as mental health problems at all. People were expected to cope with these problems on their own or seek help from family, clergymen, family physicians, or friends.

At the same time, there was a stronger sense of community. Primary support systems such as neighborhoods, churches, and extended families were more psychologically relevant and functional. They provided meaning, aid, and comfort to the individual from birth to death. There was a sense of belonging that is rare today. Of course, life was not without stress; in fact, objectively, life was probably more stressful 100 years ago than it is today. However, more people at that time were part of a larger (but not too much larger) social community that helped them to comprehend and accept those stresses. People were lonely and unhappy then as now, but there was an underlying connectedness that alleviated some of the pain and fear that now seem to accompany loneliness and depression.

Part of this sense of community was a firmer idea about what was right and wrong. The "rules of the game" were made clear. People did not necessarily follow those rules then any more than they do now; but it was clearer what the rules were and what would happen if you were caught breaking them. There were "good guys" and "bad guys," and everyone knew who they were. More important, people had a better grasp of how their social institutions worked. Whether it was a church or a store, the individual had a personal relationship with the institution and a familiarity with how it functioned that provided a greater sense of predictability and control than we experience today. Institutions then probably were not any more humane or just than they are today, but they were less mysterious and more comprehensible.

Numerous writers have discussed these changes that have occurred in our society during the last 150 years (for example, Nisbet, 1969;

Sarason, 1974). Ever since Durkheim, social scientists have been aware of how the decline in community contributes to "anomie," which in turn leads to higher rates of suicide, mental illness, crime, delinquency, marital and family conflict, and so on. Ultimately, this decline in community and the changes in attitudes and behavior that accompany it affect the rate of job stress and burnout in human service programs.

Specifically, the decline in community contributes to staff burnout in at least three different ways. First, as the social fabric unravels, the incidence of manifest psychological disorder increases, and this places an increased demand on human service programs. This increased demand eventually contributes to overload and stress for the individual providers who are expected to cope with more clients who have more problems. At the same time, other social agencies such as the police and social welfare experience the crunch and attempt to deal with it by "dumping" more of their clients onto other human service agencies, further increasing client demand.

Second, at the same time that people are experiencing more psychological distress, the informal support systems that functioned in the past are disappearing. For instance, the local cop on the beat probably did much to prevent delinquency at one time. He knew the neighborhood, he knew the youths and their parents, and he was available to provide counseling and guidance as well as law enforcement. Today, this source of psychological aid and support is gone from most communities; many others, such as the local church, do not have the same moral and psychological power they once had. Consequently, formal institutions such as mental health programs must step in more frequently and assume the burden of providing emotional support and guidance. Again, this shift in responsibility for helping ultimately means heavier case loads and more stress for practitioners.

The third consequence of the decline of community is that the public no longer has confidence in those formal institutions on which they now rely so heavily. This loss of confidence has come to include human service settings and professionals as well as other public institutions. Especially during the last 20 years, numerous events have contributed to this growing dissatisfaction and disenchantment

with formal institutions. These events include the civil rights movement; the assassinations of the Kennedys, Martin Luther King, and
Malcolm X; the Vietnam War; Watergate; and "the bomb." The
growth in malpractice suits is only one of many concrete manifesta-
tions of this disillusionment with our caregivers and our greater willingness to criticize and attack them.

An example of this increasing distrust of formal helpers recently
was provided by a special education teacher with whom I spoke. She
had been teaching special education in the public schools for 15
years, and she observed that there had been a real shift in the attitudes
of both parents and regular classroom teachers. She said that when
she began teaching, her colleagues respected and admired the work
she did. Recently, however, the regular classroom teachers with
whom she works have become more critical. They now tend to minimize her contribution. They seem to believe that the special education staff do not do a very good job and do not carry their share of the
burden. Although these attitudes are related in part to the role changes
mandated by new special education legislation (Sarason & Doris,
1979), they also are part of a larger shift in social attitudes toward
professional service providers. Professionals in many human service
fields today enjoy less public confidence and receive more public
criticism than ever before. This loss of faith in public institutions is
related to the decline in community and is another cause of increased
stress and burnout in human service programs.

Unfortunately, as the public has lost confidence in professionals,
many professionals have lost confidence in themselves. Just as the
average citizen increasingly has come to question the effectiveness
and justness of our social institutions, professionals in many fields
have become more ready to criticize and even reject the established
models of practice in their fields. For instance, community mental
health is the product of that questioning of traditional models of
practice. Although this willingness to evaluate, criticize, and change
outmoded and unfair practices is healthy and necessary, it tends to
make the day-to-day work of the practitioner more uncertain and
ambiguous. When the efficacy of the practitioner's tools comes to be
doubted, he or she finds it more difficult to experience psychological
success in the role (Chapter 3). The sense of competence becomes
elusive.

This crisis of competence caused by rapid social change and the readiness to reject past modes of practice is especially pronounced in the community mental health field. Here, more than in many other fields, practitioners have been expected to assume new roles for which they have received little training. They now must be part sociologist, part anthropologist, and part political scientist. In any given day, they may have to do delicate psychological counseling with a depressed client, give a public presentation before a community group, attend a meeting to plan a complicated program evaluation project, consult with a community group. Even in working with individual clients, the practitioner now is expected to be familiar with a variety of cultural, social, and economic factors influencing the client's life, as well as the psychodynamic issues that have traditionally been important in clinical work. And in choosing a mode of intervention with a client, the universe of alternatives has greatly expanded in recent years. Thirty years ago, psychoanalytic theory and technique dominated the field; it was the accepted mode of practice. Today, NIMH has counted over 130 different methods of psychological therapy, each claiming to be more effective than the others. Thus, as the professions themselves question what they have been doing, a crisis of competence develops for the individual practitioners which increases conflict, ambiguity, and stress in their work. However, this change in professional attitudes and practices is only part of a much larger change in our willingness to question and reject the past. Ultimately, the roots can be traced back to the decline in community and the loss of public confidence in society's institutions.

THE LEGACY OF THE SIXTIES

The decline in community and the various social consequences I have been discussing began long ago. More recently, there have been other changes in our society that not only have accelerated the decline in community but have had other effects as well, effects that ultimately have contributed to increased job stress and burnout in the human services. These changes occurred in the 1960s and have had important consequences for the way people think about the human services.

It was in the 1960s that the human services came into the public eye as never before. In the fight against racism and poverty, mental health and other human service fields were identified as primary weapons. Public support for training programs in these fields increased sharply. Being in the limelight, however, was a mixed blessing, for it meant greater public scrutiny as well as greater support for the human services.

One theme of the sixties that eventually had a profound effect on the human services was the issue of empowerment. The civil rights movement created an ethos that valued greater sharing of the franchise, greater dispersion of power, and greater participation. By the mid-sixties, community participation and community control had become cornerstones of the new social programs that were being spawned. The idea of empowerment spread quickly, and the number of groups in the political arena that desired a say over public policy greatly increased in the next few years. The consumer movement in the human services emerged at this time, creating still more turbulence in the political environment of human service programs. Gradually, the political efforts of consumer groups began to bear fruit: Demands for "accountability" led to new mechanisms of administrative control; lobbying efforts led to legislative changes, such as mandatory special education laws and community mental health laws, that dictated to a greater extent than ever before what human service professionals would do.

Thus, the idea of empowerment led to a sharp increase in the number, diversity, and power of external groups and interests trying to influence social programs. Not only has this trend reduced the professional's autonomy and control, it also has increased role conflict in human service programs. In trying to respond to diverse interests, program administrators send conflicting role demands to staff. Each new community group that is added to a program's constituency inserts a new goal that the program is expected to pursue. And each new goal leads to a new set of role demands for staff.

Today, staff members themselves have become involved in the quest for greater empowerment. Responding to what they saw as an erosion in their autonomy and power, human service workers began to unionize (Oppenheimer, 1975). Even those who resisted the pressures to form unions became more willing to challenge their employing institutions over issues of autonomy and working conditions as well as salary. In some ways, these unions may have halted the erosion of professional power; for the individual practitioner, however, the union could actually lead to yet more constraints on his or her activity. As C. Wright Mills (1951) observed long before unions became established in the white-collar world, these large and powerful labor organizations negotiate contracts with management that spell out more explicitly than ever before what workers, as well as bosses, can and cannot do. Thus, while employee unions in the human services may help to maintain the power of the workers as a group, they may lead to greater centralization and formalization in program power structures (Chapter 5). When this happens, the individual practitioner is likely to feel even more powerless.

Despite the potential threats to organizational control and autonomy that were emerging during the sixties, this was an optimistic period for the human services. New money and new programs were pouring in, and with them came great expectations. This was a period of reform, and few remained unmoved by the idealism and hope that swept the country. Most social institutions eventually were affected by this reform spirit, and mental health certainly was no exception. The influential Joint Commission on Mental Health and Mental Illness report emerged at the beginning of the decade, calling for increased public support and funding for mental health programs (1961). Two years later, Congress passed the Community Mental Health Centers Act, ushering in what was soon to be heralded as the "third revolution" in mental health.

Of course, even in the early days there were skeptics. Before many CMHCs had been established, Reiff (1966) published an article in the *American Psychologist* in which he suggested that the new mental health programs could not achieve their goals and in fact were nothing but "old wine in new bottles." Nevertheless, detractors like Reiff were clearly a minority at this time. The prevailing climate was one of hope, idealism—and naivete. This naivete was another legacy of the sixties that eventually contributed to our contemporary concern with burnout, for it led to expectations that simply could not be met. In the beginning, however, few could anticipate this. It seemed as though a "new age" had dawned for mental health and for society as a whole. Anything was possible. Of course, later analyses with the benefit of several years of history showed that "anything" was *not* possible (for example, Snow and Newton, 1976). But in the sixties, hope, excitement, and anticipation quickly overcame doubt.

By the early 1970's, it gradually became obvious that we would fall short in our efforts to achieve the social reform goals of the sixties. The new, "innovative" programs had matured; and as they did so, they lost much of the sense of mission and excitement that accompanied their creation. Cooperation gradually gave way to competition and conflict among different groups within the programs. Hope gave way to despair or cynicism. Idealism gave way to a narrow preoccupation with one's own welfare. It was in this new social climate of disillusionment and failure that the current interest in burnout was born. The wave of change that began in the sixties has ended, and its aftermath of broken promises and unfulfilled expectations has created a climate in which burnout seems rampant. Thus, the sixties gave us both the increased concern with impowerment and the great expectations that have led to much of the burnout occurring in human service programs today.

WORK AND
SELF-ACTUALIZATION

A major source of burnout in human service programs is unfulfilled expectations, and there are many historical roots of these expectations. The hope, idealism, and naivete of the reform-minded 1960s is one root. Another is the growing belief during the last 40 years that work should be more than just a paycheck, that one's job also should be a vehicle for self-fulfillment.

According to Sarason (1977), the period following World War II could aptly be named the "Age of Psychology," for people became concerned about the issues of meaning, fulfillment, and authenticity to a greater extent than ever before. There were many sources of this emerging set of values. The country had just completed an unprecedented period of deprivation, beginning with the Great Depression and continuing through the war, and people wanted to make up for lost time. Greater contact with Europe stimulated the importation of ideas such as existentialism and psychoanalysis which reinforced concern about the psychological dimensions of life. The high rate of psychiatric casualties during the war led to a massive expansion of psychiatry and clinical psychology. All of these trends contributed to this new age in which novelty, authenticity, and self-actualization became powerful values and goals.

These new values affected many areas of life. For example, people began to expect much more from sex and marriage. Increasingly, the message became that marriage was not a simple social arrangement to perpetuate the species and provide stability for the young, or even a permanent bond between two people in love; it was a vehicle for personal fulfillment. If marriage fell short of this lofty goal, it was permissible to seek divorce and a more "fulfilling" relationship. This attitude toward marriage was quite different from the earlier one which said that people should tolerate an unsatisfactory relationship as a kind of social duty. Similarly, the work of Kinsey and others gradually led to rising expectations for sex. No longer was sex seen as simply a way of producing children or a duty one spouse owed to another; now it was seen as something that was *supposed* to be fulfilling to *both* parties. The psychological, rather than biological, dimensions of sex were increasingly emphasized, and any inhibition or difficulty in performance was good cause for seeking professional help.

Work was one of those areas of life last to be affected by the Age of Psychology, but by the middle sixties attitudes about work began to change as they had about other areas of existence. Previously, a job that paid well, was secure, offered opportunities for advancement, was respected, and provided safe and pleasant working conditions was considered a very good job. Increasingly, however, many people in our society came to believe that "something more" was needed. To be truly satisfying, a job also had to provide novelty, meaning, and opportunities for creativity and personal expression. In other words, a job had to be a vehicle for self-actualization as well as economic security.

Initially, these new attitudes toward work were concentrated among the most highly educated, for those people had been most exposed to the intellectual sources of these values in their college courses. However, this new ethic came to permeate all levels of society. By the early seventies, polls revealed that even less educated, young, blue-collar workers had come to embrace these new goals and aspirations for work in unprecedented numbers (Renick & Lawler, 1978). The enormous popularity of Terkel's (1973) book, *Working,* as well as the words of the workers found between its covers, confirmed that the psychological rewards and frustrations of work had become a major cultural preoccupation.

The helping professions were not exempt from this new pursuit for meaning, novelty, and fulfillment in work. There always had been certain rewards in the professions that their members could take for granted, not the least of which was the opportunity to serve others. Security, a comfortable if not lavish income, and a high degree of respect and status also were rewards provided by most professions, and they seemed to be enough for many professionals. If they were not enough, the implication was that the problem was the dissatisfied individual. Like the individual in an unsatisfying marriage, the professional who was not happy was supposed to "pull himself together" and accept things as they were. However, today this seems to have changed. Influenced by the new norms and values of the Age of Psychology, professionals now increasingly seek novelty, authenticity, and self-actualization in their work, in addition to the other rewards pursued in the past. They tend to feel cheated if they do not find these rewards; they experience a powerful sense of longing and deprivation. Midlife career changes among professionals are occurring in unprecedented numbers as professionals leave their occupations when those occupations do not offer the new, psychological rewards that have come to be seen as essential for satisfaction (Sarason, 1977; Krantz, 1978).

Professional burnout is one more manifestation of this historical change in attitudes about work. The new values give one "permission" to experience dissatisfaction if one's work becomes tedious and lacks authenticity. Thus, the term "burnout" and the current popularity of the phenomenon, as well as the large numbers of workers in the human services who have become victims of burnout, seem to be the product of relatively new attitudes and values about life and work. The concern with self-actualization has led to new and higher expectations for work among human service workers, and these expectations contribute to the seemingly high incidence of burnout in these settings.

BURNOUT AND THE PROFESSIONAL MYSTIQUE

Thus far, I have discussed various social changes that seem to contribute to staff burnout in contemporary human service programs. However, there are other cultural factors that have been more or less constant during the last 50 years but which also contribute to the current malaise and frustration concerning work. One of the most important of these factors is a set of attitudes and beliefs concerning professionals which I have elsewhere referred to as the "professional mystique" (Cherniss et al., 1979).

Traditionally, the professions have been seen as glamorous and heroic. One only has to see how professionals such as physicians and lawyers are depicted on television to appreciate the charisma associated with the professional mystique (DeFleur, 1964). If one's only knowledge of what it is like to be a professional were based on these television melodramas, one would expect that the professional's work consists of dramatic challenges and that the professional almost always possesses the knowledge, ability, and personal qualities necessary to meet those challenges.

Unfortunately, many individuals enter a profession with just such a picture of professional work. What Lortie (1966) wrote of young lawyers probably is true for other professional groups: They begin their careers with the impression that legal work is heroic and charismatic rather than routine. For mental health professionals, the prominent image they have of mental health work before they begin their formal training probably is something akin to the image depicted in books such as *David and Lisa* or *I Never Promised You a Rose Garden:* A wise, compassionate professional confronts and gradually engages a disturbed but appealing client who, after a series of dramatic crises, emerges from the world of mental illness. Needless to say, actual work in a mental health program does not always live up to this model; and the great expectations generated in young workers by the professional mystique contribute to disillusionment and frustration.

The professional mystique is especially strong in mental health because of the field's traditional ties to the medical model. As Mendel (1978) noted, the medical model as depicted on television and in the other media emphasizes cure and success in highly dramatic, acute, and serious crises. Most actual practice, however—especially in mental health—involves ongoing work with chronic patients in which there rarely is a sense of real closure and success. Even when a "cure" seems to occur, it rarely is permanent, and frequently the professional's role in effecting it is uncertain. Especially in many of the areas associated with community mental health, such as after care, the traditional medical model of disease followed by treatment followed by cure simply is not applicable. Yet, even those workers who eschew other aspects of the medical model may embrace this aspect without even realizing it. Consequently, they become frustrated and depressed with their work and feel that they somehow have been cheated because the expected outcomes do not occur.

What are the expected outcomes generated by the professional mystique? Five seem to be especially relevant for the problem of burnout in human services. The first concerns success: An important element of the professional mystique is the belief that *credentials equal competence,* and competence leads to a high degree of success in work. Unfortunately, many human service workers, professional as well as nonprofessional, do not feel competent to handle many of the new tasks they are asked to perform. They believe that their training has been woefully deficient in many areas. Even when they feel they are performing competently, concrete success or even progress does not occur as often as they initially expected (Cherniss, 1980a; Cherniss & Egnatios, 1978a).

A second important element of the professional mystique implicated in burnout is the expectation that professional status guarantees a high level of *personal autonomy and control* in one's work. Again, as I noted in earlier chapters, the reality often is very different. A third component of the professional mystique concerns client behavior: Clients are supposed to be both *cooperative and grateful.* Fourth, the work itself is supposed to be *intrinsically interesting, meaningful, and stimulating.* Finally, relations among co-workers are expected to be *supportive and collegial.*

These elements of the professional mystique contribute to burnout in at least three ways. First, as I already suggested, the mystique creates unrealistic expectations and goals in the worker. Second, the mystique also leads to unrealistic expectations in the clients and general public. For instance, one source of the malpractice crisis in medicine was the public's belief that because physicians possess a special credential, they should not make mistakes. Of course, there were many other causes as well, but the professional mystique's effect on public expectations certainly was not insignificant. When these great expectations of the client are not fulfilled by the professional worker, the client is likely to become angry and uncooperative, and this adds to the burdens and pressures that the service provider already is experiencing.

The third way in which the professional mystique contributes to burnout is through its effect on institutional practices. Because professional work is supposed to be interesting and satisfying, there have been practically no studies of job satisfaction and morale in professionals, and supervisors and administrators in human service agencies tend to be insensitive to the quality of their staff's work life. Similarly, because professionals are supposed to be competent, orientation of new staff tends to be neglected, and the quality of supervision and in-service training varies considerably. Thus, the professional mystique is an aspect of our culture that leads to unrealistic expectations in workers, clients, administrators, and the general public. These expectations ultimately increase the pressures directed at the worker, raising the level of job stress and strain.

In addition to the general professional mystique which influences the thinking and practice of all professional and semiprofessional groups, each group tends to have its own "professional self-image" that also contributes to burnout. The professional self-image defines what is and what is not considered *real* work in that field (Prottas, 1979). For instance, police officers have an image of what real police work is. Responding to a burglary call fits that image, while mediating in a family dispute does not. Similarly, for a mental health worker, long-term psychological counseling is "real" mental health work, while helping a client find a new apartment because he is about to be evicted from his present one is not.

Human service workers bring to their work a strong desire to perform tasks that allow them to actualize their professional self-images. However, many of the tasks they are required to perform, such as paperwork, are part of a "bureaucratic self-image" that is regarded as inferior and limits their opportunities to engage in "real" work. When this occurs, the worker feels unfulfilled and is likely to become frustrated and impatient. This inability to actualize the professional self-image in human service work is a major source of dissatisfaction (Cherniss & Egnatios, 1978a) and undoubtedly contributes to burnout. However, the administrative duties that contribute to the frustration represent only one source of the problem. The worker's personal goals and preferences, strongly reinforced by the professional self-image of the worker's occupational reference group, surely contribute to the disappointment.

Thus, the larger social context is an important source of job stress and burnout in human service programs. Workers and programs function in a cultural and historical milieu that strongly shapes thought and action. The decline of community during the last 150 years has increased organizational demands on human service agencies and reduced public confidence and support in those settings. The period of rapid social change in the human services that began in the 1960s further eroded public confidence and increased political pressure and external demands. That period of reform also led to unrealistic expectations for change that inevitably gave way to disappointment, bitterness, and a greater sense of hopelessness than existed before. The growing importance of values such as authenticity, novelty, and self-actualization during this same period eventually led to new and often unrealistic demands for work; economic security and an opportunity to serve society no longer were adequate rewards for many who entered the work force. Finally, the professional mystique contributed to unrealistic expectations concerning work in human service programs.

In the last four chapters, I have identified a number of factors in the work organization, the individual, and the larger social and historical milieu that seem to contribute to staff burnout in human service programs. But what can be done about the problem? What kinds of interventions are suggested by this analysis of the causes of burnout? Although there are no panaceas, previous experience in different kinds of settings does suggest a number of strategies for combating burnout that could be adopted in human service programs.

Chapter 9

PREVENTING BURNOUT

For those who work in human service programs, research and analysis on job stress and burnout are not enough. Burnout is a problem that staff deal with daily, both in their own setting and in those they consult with. Even though the current state of our knowledge should make one cautious about intervening, the fact is that staff do intervene, even when they are not conscious of doing so. They make decisions and take actions that affect job stress for themselves, their co-workers, and other caregivers in the community. Thus, it is important to use whatever knowledge and insight we have to plan the most constructive policies and programs for reducing burnout in the human services.

SOME GENERAL GUIDELINES
FOR INTERVENTION

Before considering specific steps that can be taken to deal with job stress and burnout, some general guidelines need to be noted. First, while the research and analysis presented in previous chapters is incomplete and uncertain in many respects, it represents the firmest basis for intervention. Whatever is done to alleviate burnout in a setting should be based on empirical analysis and the most plausible theory. Thus, in formulating procedures for dealing with burnout, what is known about the underlying dynamics should guide one's efforts. To briefly recapitulate, burnout is a particular coping response to stress and strain experienced in the job. Stress occurs when there is an imbalance between job demands and the worker's resources (skills, abilities, time, energy) for meeting them. The worker's personal goals and preferences also create demands that can lead to stress and strain. Therefore, interventions to alleviate burnout can take four different tacks: (1) reduce or eliminate external job demands; (2) change personal goals, preferences, and expectations; (3) increase the worker's resources for meeting the demands; (4) or provide coping substitutes for the withdrawal characteristic of burnout.

A second guideline concerns the level of intervention. Although factors contributing to burnout can be found at the level of the individual, the work setting, and the larger social historical context, the most useful point of intervention is the job and work setting. It is easier to restructure a role than to restructure the character of either an individual or a society. Obviously, the problem cannot be completely eliminated until individuals and the society in which they live are changed, but much can be done before this occurs simply by changing the structure of roles, power, and norms in human service organizations.

A third guideline concerns the importance of prevention. Once burnout develops in an organization, it is highly contagious; also, when even one staff person burns out, reversing the condition often requires a sustained effort. The laboratory provides a vivid lesson: in his research on learned helplessness (see Chapter 3), Seligman (1975) found that once an animal developed the syndrome, literally hundreds of retraining trials might be necessary before the effects were extinguished and the animal once again responded adaptively. In other words, learned helplessness and burnout tend to be self-perpetuating, and it is difficult to reverse them once they are established. Thus, prevention is far more effective and less costly than treatment, and preventive interventions should be emphasized. In addition, if one must deal with burnout in a setting after it has become well established, one must be prepared for a long-term effort that may not initially yield observable results. In alleviating burnout that has become widespread and entrenched, one must adopt a long time perspective. Otherwise, those who are attempting to alleviate burnout may burn out themselves.

Another important guideline for intervention is that one should avoid the tendency to define solutions in terms of "more resources." Clearly, role overload is a common cause of burnout in many human service agencies, and doubling the number of staff, drastically reducing the staff/client ratio, and substantially increasing funding levels can help reduce overload. However, the tendency to define the solution as "more resources" has some serious flaws. There are many other causes of burnout (such as role conflict and ambiguity, lack of variety, lack of autonomy and control over one's work, and destructive institutional norms) that have little to do with resources. Also, research has suggested that relatively large changes in staff/client ratios are necessary before any substantial change in staff burnout occurs (Berkeley Planning Associates, 1977). Thus, to take one example, reducing class sizes from 30 to 25 or even 20 students probably will not substantially reduce role overload and burnout in classroom teachers, although many teachers think that it would. Finally, focusing all of one's efforts on gaining more resources for a program as a way of alleviating job stress is misguided because obtaining the additional resources often is problematic. Fortunately, in any human service setting, much can be done to reduce burnout without any substantial increase in resources.

The last guideline for intervention concerns the importance of awareness: "Consciousness-raising" must be the first step in any effort to deal with the problem of burnout in a community agency. If supervisors and administrators minimize the problem, if they are not aware of the negative effects of burnout for staff, clients, and agencies, and if they do not realize the extent to which the structure of the work setting contributes to the problem, then little can be done to alleviate job stress and burnout in a setting. Thus, becoming aware of and knowledgeable about the problem and helping others to do so as well are the first steps that must be taken in any effort to deal with burnout.

Given these general guidelines, there are five possible points of intervention in any human service agency: staff development, the job and role structure, management development, organizational problem-solving and decision-making, and program goals and guiding philosophies. Numerous initiatives are possible in each area, and one often can launch efforts simultaneously in several of them.

Staff Development Interventions

Many of the underlying causes of job stress and burnout can be attacked through relatively modest staff development programs. For instance, we know that much job stress in human service fields is caused by the excessive demands workers impose on themselves. The new worker tends to bring unrealistically high goals to the job, such as "curing" all schizophrenic clients in an after-care program. When the worker fails to achieve these goals, he or she often abandons them and adopts the most minimal custodial goals. Through carefully designed staff development programs, workers can be helped to become more aware of what their personal goals are in order to alleviate the problem of unrealistically high or low expectations.

Workers also can be helped to adopt new goals that might provide alternative sources of gratification. For instance, teachers in inner-city schools who often are frustrated in their attempts to bring about rapid academic progress in their students can be helped to recognize other goals for their work, such as increasing the students' self-esteem or interpersonal skills. Also, staff in community agencies can be helped to see the potential dangers of becoming too dependent on work for need-fulfillment and to develop alternative sources of gratification outside the job. Thus, by focusing on the workers' goals, staff development programs can help reduce the internal demands staff impose on themselves which contribute to job stress and burnout in community settings.

Orientation of new workers represents one particular point at which worker goals and expectations can be influenced. For instance, one company successfully reduced "reality shock" and turnover in its sales personnel by providing new workers with a booklet that described typical examples of the kinds of frustrations and disappointments they might encounter in the job (Weitz, 1956). The company had previously used an orientation booklet that accentuated the positive, based on the assumption that new workers would be scared away if they were exposed to the difficulties and problems in the beginning. However, the workers who received the "realistic" booklet actually were more likely to remain than were those who received the positive booklet.

A particularly effective approach to orientation in a human service setting is used by many public health nursing units (Cherniss, 1980a). When new nurses are hired, they are not initially assigned any clients. Instead, they attend various seminars and workshops and accompany experienced nurses on their rounds. Gradually, the new nurses begin to assume more responsibility, working with patients themselves while being observed by more experienced nurses. These "field advisors" are not the nurses' formal supervisors. Orientation and supervision functions are separated. Eventually the nurses assume total responsibility for a regular case load and work on their own. This kind of careful orientation of new workers eliminates much of the ambiguity and concern about performance that contribute to burnout. Expectations for competence initially are modest, minimizing the extent to which the nurses feel that they are not performing as they should.

Sometimes, however, the problem is not excessively ambitious goals but difficulty in recognizing goal attainment, and here staff development efforts can be useful as well. For instance, staff in an experimental treatment program for chronic schizophrenics were helped to overcome much frustration through the development of a monitoring and feedback system that was sensitive to small gains in treatment with this population (Colarelli & Siegal, 1966). Staff members participated in the development of the system, and much staff development time was allocated to helping them become proficient in its use. This kind of mechanism reduced some of the ambiguity that makes work in the human services so difficult and unrewarding and increased the degree to which staff experienced psychological success in their work.

A more obvious and direct way to increase psychological success is to help staff increase their skill and ability in their work. In-service training programs that provide opportunities to learn new techniques for working with client problems, to refine old techniques, or to develop greater theoretical sophistication in diagnosis and treatment can help alleviate stress as well as increase staff effectiveness.

A particularly useful focus for training is conflict resolution and organizational problem-solving. Much of the frustration and stress that occur in human service staff is a response to conflict between their needs or goals and the demands of the organization (professional-bureaucratic role conflict). When these conflicts occur, staff often feel helpless because they know little about how the system works and have not acquired skills for negotiating it. Conflicts with supervisors, co-workers, and personnel in other systems also are an important source of job stress in the human services, and, again, most staff lack the knowledge and skill that could help them feel more competent in handling these conflicts. Kramer (1974) developed for nurses a successful training program in organizational problem-solving and conflict resolution which could serve as a model for programs in other human service systems as well. She designed the program by collecting examples of typical organizational conflicts and frustrations from experienced nurses in the field. She also asked the most organizationally adept and successful nurses how they would handle those incidents. These problems and solutions then formed the basis of the training program for novices. Kramer found that new nurses who were exposed to this program experienced less role strain and maintained their initial idealism and commitment to a greater extent than did a control group.

In general, in-service training can be used to provide staff with many kinds of coping skills. Conflict resolution and organizational problem-solving probably are the most useful, but there are many others as well. For instance, training designed to help staff budget and plan their time more efficiently might be especially valuable as a way of helping them to cope with role overload. However, whatever the focus, in-service training should be directed to making staff more aware of the causes and symptoms of burnout. Increased awareness of the problem is essential for preventing it from becoming severe; for once staff are aware of the problem, they often can monitor job stress and strain in their work situation and act before it becomes excessive and leads to the maladaptive withdrawal and apathy associated with burnout.

Although training is a useful way to increase staff awareness and coping skill, it should be supplemented with other staff development methods that serve a similar function. One of the other methods is the "burnout checkup" (Mendel, 1978). Periodically, (for instance, every six months) each staff member meets with a staff development specialist for the purpose of assessing current sources of frustration, stress, and satisfaction in work. The staff member is helped to assess how job pressures might be affecting attitudes and performance. The findings of the assessment are used to make changes in the staff person's job that enhance rewarding aspects and reduce unrewarding ones.

When staff begin to react adversely to job stress, counseling with a focus on one's response to work represents another potentially valuable staff development method. This counseling is similar to "consultee-centered consultation" (Caplan, 1970), and its use in combating burnout has been described especially well by Schwartz and Will (1961). In their example, the authors successfully dealt with an "epidemic" of burnout on a ward of a psychiatric hospital through a series of interviews with one of the nurses. The nurse was encouraged to ventilate her feelings and to adopt an "attitude of inquiry" toward her negative reactions to patients and co-workers. Although initially resistant to the intervention, the nurse gradually "opened up," and within six sessions her attitudes dramatically improved. This counseling approach not only reduced burnout in the nurse who was the target of the intervention, but also the other nursing staff seemed to respond positively through a "chain reaction" effect.

Although individual counseling or consultation can help alleviate the negative effects of job stress, group interventions probably are even more potentially valuable. There are many institutional barriers to social interaction and support among staff in human service settings that must be overcome (see Chapter 6), but if one can overcome these, the potential benefits are great. Many staff members in community programs tend to feel that their reactions are unique. They rarely have an opportunity to discuss their work-related feelings and problems with others in a setting that encourages both emotional support and positive problem-solving. Through carefully planned and skillfully run support groups, staff in these settings can be helped to cope adaptively with the stress associated with their jobs.

One final staff development mechanism that has been discussed recently in the literature is the "resource exchange network" (Sarason & Lorentz, 1979). An example of the formation of such a network occurred at a conference where three nurses from a Visiting Nurse Association, a university person interested in research on self-help groups, and a person from a state agency on alcoholism came together in a group. The group leader asked the nurses, "To what extent is alcoholism a problem in the homes you go into?" As the nurses responded, the person from the state became aware of how he and the nurses could be of help to one another. The group leader then asked the nurses, "To what extent are you dealing with problems of self-help, such as diabetics, physically impaired, and so on?" In this instance, the university researcher and the nurses quickly saw how they could help each other further their interests and cope with problems they were confronting in their work. Through experiences such as these, workers in the human services can receive concrete help that reduces the burdens of their jobs. Also, their horizons are broadened as they come to know people involved in different settings working with different kinds of problems. Finally, just the process of sharing information and exchanging resources reduces the sense of isolation that so often characterizes work in the human services. Individuals who participate in such networks experience a sense of community and participation that increases their sense of efficacy, renews hope and optimism, and counteracts the sense of helplessness that contributes to burnout. Thus, staff development initiatives that encourage the formation of resource exchange networks among staff within an organization and across different organizations in the community represent yet another way of alleviating job stress and burnout.

To summarize, staff development efforts can reduce the incidence of staff burnout in a setting in several ways. They can help staff to adopt more realistic goals and develop alternative sources of gratification outside of work. They can help staff develop new goals for their work that provide alternative sources of gratification. They also can help reduce role ambiguity and increase psychological success by helping staff to develop and use personal monitoring and feedback mechanisms in their work. Finally, staff development can help by providing staff with knowledge and skills that increase their effectiveness in handling both the specific tasks associated with their roles and the more general interpersonal conflicts and problems that tend to occur in any large, formal organization. Several mechanisms for implementing these staff development goals are available, including orientation programs, burnout checkups, counseling or consultation, support groups, and resource exchange networks. Of course, the more common staff development mechanisms found in human service settings—in-service training and supervision—also provide arenas in which the factors contributing to job stress and burnout can be addressed. Ultimately, staff development interventions probably will be limited in their benefits because they do not directly affect the structural causes of role strain and job stress. However, staff development in some situations can do much to alleviate the negative consequences of that stress.

Changing the Job

The structure of roles in a program represents a second major point of intervention for the alleviation of staff burnout. The role structure of a program (see Chapter 5) is malleable. Although the division of labor usually is not made with job stress and the growth needs of staff in mind, these factors can be taken into consideration. Jobs and roles can be structured in ways that reduce stress and enhance personal fulfillment for the role players.

In considering the role structure of a human service program as a point of intervention, some general guidelines should be kept in mind. First, job stress has two basic sources: external demands that exceed the individual's resources, and lack of opportunity to do the kind of work that is most interesting and rewarding. One can change the job to reduce role overload, ambiguity, and conflict, but one also should consider ways of enriching the job—that is, increasing opportunities for variety, stimulation, learning, and meaning. The second guideline is that one must always be sensitive and responsive to the individual needs and preferences of the workers who will perform the roles. A role that is stimulating and meaningful for one individual will not necessarily be so for another. Similarly, what is excessively demanding for one worker may not be for another. As much as possible, roles and role structures in a program should be flexible to accommodate the strengths and preferences of those who work in them. One should not always start with a fixed job or role and then make the worker fit the job. Instead, one should try to fit the job to the worker whenever possible.

The last guideline is related to the previous one: Do not expect a worker to be good at everything. In designing roles and assigning workers to them, identify each worker's strengths and then place the worker in a role that emphasizes those strengths. When these three guidelines are kept in mind, a number of specific options for changing jobs and role structures are available.

CLIENT RESPONSIBILITY

The most obvious way in which staff roles can be changed to reduce job stress is through the assignment of responsibility for clients. The delivery of service to clients is the major activity of a human service program; it is here that much burnout is created, and it is here that much can be done to prevent burnout. Three actions appear to be especially useful.

First, one can limit the number of clients for whom staff are responsible at any one time. This idea is especially important for worker settings, such as after care, day care, group homes, and public education, in which staff work with groups of clients. In one study of child care settings, Maslach and Pines (1977) found that without changing the staff/child ratio, the degree of overload experienced by staff could be greatly reduced simply by restricting the number of children for whom a staff person was responsible. For instance, suppose that a program has 12 children and three staff. Staff can share the responsibility for the 12 children or they can each take responsibility for four. Maslach and Pines found that there was less role overload when responsibility was divided. Even though the staff/ child ratio was no different, there was less stress when the group was divided into three smaller groups and staff were assigned to these. This role structure probably also contributed to a closer and more meaningful relationship between the staff members and the children to whom they were assigned. Also, the staff probably felt a greater sense of personal responsibility, autonomy, and control when they were solely responsible for a smaller subgroup of children. Thus, for a number of reasons, limiting the number of clients for whom staff are responsible at one time appears to be an effective way of reducing stress in a community program.

One also can prevent burnout by carefully selecting the mix of clients assigned to staff. In general, one should avoid assigning several of the most difficult clients to staff. In any program, certain types of clients will be considered tacitly the "dirty work" of the agency (Maslach, 1976). These are the clients who are the more difficult to work with, who tend to have less successful outcomes, or who are physically or morally repugnant. Dying patients, resistant and abusive clients, and the most severely handicapped fall into this category. In community mental health programs, the after-care clients typically are regarded as the least rewarding and desirable to work with. In programs for the mentally retarded, it is the more acting out, more intellectually handicapped, or less physically attractive clients who are regarded as the least desirable. In many community agencies, any member of a "multiproblem family" tends to be placed in this category. Unfortunately, programs often are organized so that certain staff spend an excessive amount of their time with these more difficult clients. This situation is fine for the other staff, and there may be a few who prefer to work with the less "popular" clients. However, this arrangement will usually lead to high levels of burnout for those who work with these clients.

An approach that is fairer and less conducive to burnout is to distribute the difficult clients evenly among the staff. In agencies where there are several programs, burnout can be reduced by having every staff person work in at least two different programs. When this policy was adopted in a regional center for the mentally retarded, staff members who spent part of the day working with the least rewarding clients were able to spend the rest of the day working with more rewarding ones (Sarason et al., 1971). The burden of caring for the most severely retarded was shared, and, as a result, burnout within the center was reduced. This staffing policy also had additional benefits: Variety was greater for staff than it would be if they were confined to only one program, and there was less rivalry and competition among programs within the agency because all staff felt a sense of loyalty to more than one program.

This general approach can be extended to include the daily scheduling of staff. Job stress will more likely remain within manageable proportions if staff are encouraged to arrange each day so that the rewarding and unrewarding activities are alternated and balanced. Concentrating all of the unrewarding activities together, either at the end or beginning of the day, increases stress. Unfortunately, there always will be unrewarding activities that must be performed and difficult clients who must be helped in human service programs; and these activities and clients will contribute to stress and frustration. However, the role structure of a program usually can be designed in a way that mixes and balances the "dirty work" of the agency. When this is done, the incidence of burnout is greatly reduced.

TIME-OUTS AND RELIEF

Even when client responsibility is organized in a way that minimizes stress, the staff role in a community setting is a difficult one. Over time, emotional strain increases and reaches excessive levels. However, several ways of alleviating the burden are available. First, roles should be structured in a way that allows workers to take "time-outs" whenever necessary. Most jobs in the human services allow little opportunity for the reflection and thought that are necessary for effective coping. Time-outs that allow staff to escape temporarily from the demands of the role and to think, uninterrupted, about what they are doing would do much to reduce overload and strain.

One way of ensuring that time-outs will be available for staff is to utilize auxiliary personnel such as paraprofessionals and volunteers. By now, the idea of paraprofessionals is a familiar one in the human services. However, the rationales for using paraprofessionals usually involve economic and clinical considerations. Their potential value as a way of reducing job stress and burnout for other staff has not been emphasized. Paraprofessionals can be utilized in a way that gives professional staff opportunities for time-outs. Also, paraprofessionals can help reduce the overload problem experienced by so many agencies simply by increasing the number of staff resources. Finally, utilization of paraprofessionals can open up new role possibilities for professionals. When they become supervisors, trainers, and program coordinators, professional staff can experience increased amounts of responsibility, status, variety, and learning in their own work.

Vacation time policies also can be used to provide relief when it is needed. Employees should be encouraged to take frequent vacations. The tendency to allow vacation time to accumulate and to regard this as some kind of "status symbol" should be discouraged. Flexibility should be maximized so that workers can take vacation time on short notice whenever needed.

A related recommendation is that supervisors limit the number of hours a person works. There are staff members who seem to take pride and satisfaction in working ten or twelve hours a day. The long-term consequences of this kind of total inolvement in one's work can be deleterious for both the staff person and others. Such heroic behavior should be discouraged.

One final suggestion concerns agency policies regarding part-time employment. In our society, the 40-hour week has become the norm; however, there is nothing sacred or inherently beneficial about this arrangement. In fact, for especially demanding work such as that found in community programs, the 40-hour week may be detrimental. Unfortunately, in many instances there are strong disincentives to working less than 40 hours per week. For instance, a 42-year-old mother of two, married to another professional, worked in a mental health program as a clinical social worker. She preferred to work half-time in order to have more time for her family and other interests. However, to do so would have meant she would lose all her fringe benefits (health insurance, retirement, vacation benefits, and so on). Even then, she might have worked half-time if she had been allowed. However, she was not even given the choice. She and her co-workers were told that they must work full-time or not at all. In this and most other work settings, "full-time" meant 40 hours per week. These disincentives to part-time work contribute to staff burnout in community agencies and should be eliminated. Staff who wish to work part-time should be allowed or even encouraged to do so.

OPPORTUNITIES FOR CREATING NEW PROGRAMS

Thus far, many of the recommendations have concerned ways in which the role structure could be changed in order to reduce excessive demands and overload. However, the role structure also can be modified to provide opportunities for personal and professional growth. One particularly effective way of doing this is to make the creation of new programs part of every staff role.

A good example of how the opportunity for creating new programs was built into the role of every staff person is the Residential Youth Center (RYC) described by Goldenberg (1971). The RYC was created to serve troubled adolescents and their families. It was located in the inner city and served a clientele that came from this milieu. The staff were primarily indigenous paraprofessionals. Preventing burnout was a major concern from the beginning, and one way in which the RYC attempted to do this was to encourage each staff member (including secretary, cook, director, and live-in counselors) to develop and run his or her own "evening program." These programs were offered to the residents, their families, and people from the community; they could be anything that the staff person was interested in pursuing. Not surprisingly, the variety of programs was great. One staff member offered group therapy. Another taught karate. Still another developed a wood shop and taught woodworking to anyone who was interested. The important thing about these evening programs was that they provided the staff with an opportunity to conceive, plan, and implement their *own* program. They could experience the joy of creating in a way that was not possible in any other part of their job. Of course, most of the programs that were created also provided valuable experiences for clients and community members. However, the evening program idea was primarily intended as a vehicle for enhancing creative expression for the staff. Such an arrangement can go a long way toward maintaining commitment and involvement in staff working in demanding human service roles.

CAREER LADDERS

One final idea for alleviating burnout through the role structure involves the use of career ladders in a work setting. The lack of career ladders has been identified as a major source of dissatisfaction in paraprofessionals; however, in many community settings, even the professional staff are deprived of the personal gratifications that result when one's accomplishments and professional growth are recognized through increases in responsibility and status. In fact, in fields such as teaching, practitioners remain in the same status unless they go into administration. To do so usually means an end to the person's career as a practitioner.

Career stages can help alleviate burnout by enhancing the practitioner's precarious sense of competence (see Chapter 3). As Lortie wrote:

> Status channels the flow of deference to individuals. Deference can reassure people of their worth and competence; moving through a series of statuses therefore provides a gradient of increasing psychological support. Repeated indications of other's respect can quell self-doubt. Deference, in short, can help people who work with uncertainty and ambiguity [Lortie, 1975: 161].

Career stages also tend to increase an individual's commitment and motivation by providing concrete goals to strive for. Each increase in status gives one an enormous sense of accomplishment. It also tends to increase the person's commitment to and identification with the field. To quote Lortie again:

> Staged careers produce cycles of effort, attainment, and renewed ambition. In tying the individual to the occupation, they give him a stake in its future. Staging gives reality and force to the idea of the future; it generates effort, ambition, and identification with the occupation [1975: 85].

Thus any way in which career stages can be built into the role structure of a human service program will probably help alleviate burnout. Yearly "merit" raises that are usually given automatically are not enough. A true career ladder requires advancement in the form of meaningful increases in responsibility, privileges, and status. Advancement should be regarded as a reward for good work and a recognition that the individual is capable of doing more than he or she has done in the past. However, care should be taken that the career ladder does not become a rigid "class structure." Advancement should be a real possibility for all workers. When workers feel that the higher stages are beyond their reach, the career ladder becomes an added source of stress and frustration. As with other aspects of the role structure I have discussed, the career ladder can contribute to burnout or alleviate burnout. It all depends on how it is used.

Management Development Interventions

A third and especially important point of intervention is the supervisory level of an agency. In Chapter 6, I noted that supervision and leadership strongly influence the organizational climate of an agency. Research has suggested that differences in the quality of supervision and leadership account for more of the variance in burnout than any other single factor. Also, intervention in other areas such as staff development and change in the role structure usually requires the active support and leadership of agency administration. Thus, in any effort to alleviate burnout, some attention should be given to the managerial level.

There are three basic causes of poor supervision and leadership in human service agencies: attitudes, lack of skill, and excessive role demands. Some supervisors and administrators act in ways that increase job stress for subordinates because they are not aware of the consequences of their actions. Other administrators contribute to burnout in their employees because they simply do not know how to manage. However, many other administrators fail because of the constant conflicts and demands that *their* superiors impose on them. Management development to alleviate burnout may need to address any or all of these three basic causes of inadequate supervision and administrative behavior.

In-service training for current management personnel and pre-service training for future managers represent the most obvious management development interventions. Many individuals who become administrators in mental health, education, corrections, and other human service fields receive surprisingly little preparation for their work. The underlying assumption seems to be that if one is a competent practitioner, one will be an effective administrator. Of course, experience repeatedly shows this assumption to be wrong. Nevertheless, the human services have lagged behind the private-industrial sector in their sensitivity to the need for management training. Thus, it is not surprising that many supervisors and administrators in community agencies lack the skills necessary for effective role performance. One obvious intervention is to provide training programs for individuals who are about to move into administrative positions to prepare them for handling aspects of the job that managers tend to have the most difficulty with. These aspects include disorganization, inability to cope with workers' anger or other stressful situations, inability to set priorities, and problems in handling authority.

Training for both future and current managers also can be used as a vehicle for changing attitudes toward leadership and burnout that may contribute to poor organizational climates. Administrators cannot be "brainwashed," nor should one attempt to do so. However, administrators can and should be helped to become more aware of their own operational philosophy of management, alternative approaches and philosophies, and what is known about the consequences of different approaches. They also should be helped to become aware of the problem of job stress and burnout and the potential effects of burnout on worker performance. In-service training programs can perform these valuable functions.

However, training frequently is not sufficient by itself. The best students may prove to be the worst practitioners. I became aware of this fact recently when a student of mine complained about the head of a local community program in which she was an employee. She described her boss as arbitrary, dictatorial, and extremely demanding. Although this student may have been distorting or exaggerating and may have contributed to the problems herself, my previous contacts with her led me to doubt that this was the case. What was both troubling and illuminating about her account was that the administrator whom she was describing was a former student of mine. In fact, he was one of the most able and enthusiastic students I have ever had. I would have thought that he would be an especially sensitive and skillful administrator based on the attitudes he expressed in class and the principles he seemed to acquire. This incident confirmed, however, that changes in attitude and knowledge which occur during training may not be sufficent for producing the desired behavior in a supervisory role.

One method for dealing with this problem is the use of ongoing monitoring and feedback mechanisms for managers. Research has suggested that when supervisors receive feedback on their supervisory performance from their subordinates, their performance often changes in positive ways. Just as line staff often receive little feedback, positive or negative, on their performance, so administrators also receive little feedback. They may have mastered the concepts of good management in a training program or by reading a book, but without ongoing feedback on their performance they have no way of knowing whether they are following those concepts in their day-to-day behavior.

Hegarty (1974) described a study which showed that feedback can be used to improve managerial behavior. Subordinates were given survey questionnaires which asked them to evaluate the performance of their superiors on a number of dimensions. The workers also were given the opportunity to indicate what they most valued and desired in a boss. The surveys were anonymous, and only the supervisors saw the results. When another survey was conducted a few months later, the results suggested that the supervisors who received feedback had changed in positive ways.

More recent research has suggested that this "survey feedback" technique is a complex one that will be more or less effective depending upon how it is used. For instance, one study evaluated the effects of different types of feedback on the supervisory performance of school principals (Burns, 1977). Teachers were asked to complete a survey in which they indicated what the ideal principal would be like and then evaluated how closely their own principal resembled the ideal. One group of principals received both the "ideal" and the "real" ratings, but another group received only the "real" ratings and another group received only the "ideal" ratings. A fourth group received no feedback at all. When the survey was readministered, the results suggested that the principals who received only the "ideal" ratings improved more than did those who received both the "real" and the "ideal" ratings or the "real" ratings alone. However, all of the feedback groups showed significantly more improvement than the group that received no feedback. There is no way of knowing whether these results are generally valid for other work settings; however, they suggest that different formats for providing managerial personnel with feedback from subordinates may be differentially effective. Of course, the results also confirm the general notion that feedback can be used to improve managerial performance in human service settings.

Unfortunately, there will be some instances in which poor supervision is the result of managerial stress. Just as job stress can impede the performance of line staff, so, too, can it deleteriously affect the performance of managers. Middle-level administrators in human service programs are especially vulnerable to role conflict and ambiguity. Stress and strain is built into their roles. Also, the extent to which the job provides opportunities for need fulfillment varies for managers as it does for other workers. When a manager feels he or she is treading water, that the work does not provide opportunities for learning, variety, challenge, and meaning, his or her attitudes and behavior toward subordinates may be adversely affected.

I recently came upon an example of how role demands and pressures can influence a supervisor's functioning. In a residential treatment program for youth, the much-liked and respected individual who had directed the program for many years recently resigned. He was replaced by someone hired from the outside who quickly began to confront serious "morale" problems. I was asked by the new director to assess the problems and make recommendations to her. In interviewing the staff and new director, the following picture emerged. The new director had recently gone through a painful divorce. She felt that she was in some way responsible and was dealing with the feelings of failure and guilt. Her self-esteem had received a severe blow. Also, she felt that she had not done well in two previous jobs. Thus, she was under great pressure to "prove" to herself and others that she was a capable administrator. She confessed that if she "failed" in this new role, she believed that her career probably would be finished.

The pressure was made even greater because the new director had replaced someone who was unusually popular with the staff. The old director had emphasized nurturance and support in his supervision of staff. According to one staff member whom I interviewed, "With the old director, we always felt that we were competent, that in his eyes we could do no wrong. He really seemed to care about us." Under the helm of the easy-going former director, the program had not changed or grown very much, and there were many administrative problems. However, his "human relations" approach to management had produced a positive social climate and a high degree of cohesion among the staff. Without doubt, his was a hard act to follow.

Not surprisingly, the new director soon began to experience difficulty in her dealings with the staff, especially the older ones. Her style of management was very different from her predecessor's. She wanted to "make a splash," to expand and improve current programs, and to develop new ones. Her superior also wanted to see growth and improvement in the center. The new director valued order and organization more than her predecessor had, and she wanted to maintain a high degree of control over the staff in order to ensure that the program would function at a high level. The staff increasingly resented her attempts to reduce their autonomy. They believed that the new director did not trust them and questioned their competence. Several went over the new director's head and complained to her immediate superior. The new director believed that her boss was too inclined to side with the staff and that she did not have his complete confidence and support. She became isolated, angry, and anxious. As the situation deteriorated, she tended to increase her efforts to control and provided even less support to the staff. Everyone's morale suffered.

In this example, the new director was under great pressure, and this pressure seemed to adversely affect her performance as a supervisor for the staff. Recent events in both personal and professional spheres of her life contributed to a high fear of failure and strong internal demands to succeed in her new role. The popularity of her predecessor created high expectations for the new director in the minds of her staff and superior. Although management training might have helped to better prepare this new director, the emotional conflicts created by various role pressures probably would still interfere with her judgment and performance. In this and many other situations, only a reduction of the pressures and demands associated with this particular role at this particular point in time would improve the supervisory behavior of the new director. Her own goals would have to change as well as the expectations and preferences of her subordinates and superior. Thus, management development programs designed to alleviate organizational stress and burnout often must consider the role pressures directed at supervisory personnel as well as their level of awareness and skill.

Organizational Problem-Solving and Decision-Making

No matter how well structured and managed a program might be, problems and conflicts in a human service organization are inevitable. Unfortunately, few human service programs have built-in mechanisms for dealing with interpersonal and organizational difficulties. Consequently, when dissatisfaction and problems do occur, they often fester for a long time until reaching a crisis when administrative intervention cannot be put off. When problems are handled in an atmosphere of crisis and urgency, the solutions often are far from ideal. Today's solutions often become tomorrow's problems when organizational problem-solving occurs in this ad hoc fashion. Thus, a fourth point of intervention for alleviating burnout is organizational problem-solving and conflict resolution.

Much already is known about decision-making, problem-solving, and conflict resolution in organizations, and there is much more that we do not know about this important topic. Several good, practical books are available (such as Maier, 1963; Filley, 1975), and I would urge the interested reader to consult them. In considering the relevance of this issue for the alleviation of burnout, there are three general recommendations that seem to be particularly useful.

First, community programs should create formal mechanisms for group and organizational conflict resolution and problem-solving. In one after-care program I worked with, such a mechanism developed spontaneously. One of the staff had attended a workshop on job stress and burnout, and she offered to make a presentation to the staff on what she had learned. During the discussion that followed her presentation, she suggested that it might be interesting and useful to conduct a survey to find out what staff liked and did not like about their work setting. The head of the program as well as the other staff members were enthusiastic about the idea, as long as the results could be shared with everyone and anonymity protected the respondents. The survey was conducted and another meeting was held to present the findings and discuss them. Although the survey showed that staff were generally satisfied with their jobs and liked many things about the program, there also were some problems. The staff continued to meet regularly to discuss these problems and develop recommendations for dealing with them. The staff member who began the process continued to assume primary leadership for it; she ran the meetings and took responsibility for any coordination necessary between meetings. The head of the program supported these efforts; she regularly attended the meetings and did not try to argue with or contradict staff when they offered criticisms. She also considered the recommendations that emerged from this process and implemented most of them. Most important of all, this self-corrective problem-solving process became a regular, institutionalized part of this program. The staff survey was administered every six months and each time there followed a series of meetings in which problems were addressed. This mechanism seemed to be an effective way in which job stress was prevented from reaching intolerable levels.

A second general recommendation concerns staff training. For group problem-solving and conflict resolution mechanisms to be effective, it is important that the staff involved possess the necessary skills. Thus, as I already have suggested, there should be in-service training in group problem-solving and conflict resolution for as many members as possible. When staff have both the opportunity and the skills necessary for effective planning and problem-solving, many of the causes of organizational burnout can be alleviated before they ever reach critical levels.

The third recommendation concerns decision-making and the program's "power structure" (see Chapter 5). There has been much debate over the years about the desirability of participative decision-making in human service programs (Raskin, 1973; Cherniss & Egnatios, 1978b). Although there is much research to suggest that increased levels of staff autonomy and participation contribute to better decisions, less conflict, and higher morale, it is clear that in certain areas it will be difficult to share administrative responsibility widely among staff. Thus, the amount of participation that is optimal will depend upon the situation. However, it is generally desirable for administrators to maximize staff participation in decision-making. In some areas of program functioning, this may mean giving each staff member total autonomy. In other areas, it may mean that decisions will be made collectively by the staff. In still other areas, the administration may need to retain final authority. However, even in these areas, it is possible to use advisory group structures that enable staff to study the issues and present recommendations for the administration to consider.

A good example of this last approach to increasing staff participation was described by Reppucci and Saunders (1975). A reformatory for boys was riddled with corruption, inefficiency, and public scandal. The director finally was fired and a new person brought in from the outside to replace him. Within a month after he arrived on the scene, the new director sent a memo to all staff outlining the problems he had identified and inviting them to propose solutions. He indicated that several discussion groups and task forces would be formed in which staff would be able to consider the problems and develop recommendations for dealing with them. He would then consider the recommendations and implement those that seemed most desirable. About 60 percent of the staff ultimately participated in the process, and the program of institutional reform that eventually was adopted came from recommendations that emerged from these groups. In this situation, the director could not escape from or delegate away the responsibility that was his. In a crisis situation, the head of an organization must take decisive action and accept responsibility for whatever happens. It is not reasonable to expect an administrator in such a situation to give up his authority to others when he is the one who will be held accountable. However, it is both possible and desirable for the administrator to actively encourage and use input from staff. Doing so not only helps to secure greater support from the staff (who ultimately can make or break an administrator), but it also frequently produces better decisions and policies than the administrator would develop alone or in consultation with a few close "lieutenants."

Thus, complete staff control and autonomy in a human service program may not always be either possible or desirable. However, organizational stress will be reduced when staff are involved in decision-making as much as possible.

Agency Goals and Guiding Philosophies

Interventions that alleviate burnout by focusing on agency goals follow directly from the discussion of the normative structure's impact on organizational burnout (Chapter 5). Human service programs differ in the degree to which their goals are clear, consistent, and realistic. Burnout will tend to be less severe in settings where the goals are unambiguous, clearly prioritized to minimize apparent conflict, and attainable.

Burnout also seems to be less severe in programs where there is a strong sense of shared purpose. Thus, program leadership should consider ways in which a strong sense of purpose can be developed and maintained. According to Reppucci (1973), the development of a guiding philosophy of treatment or service is a particularly effective mechanism for creating a sense of purpose. Clark's (1970) work suggests that the more distinctive the guiding philosophy, the more effective it will be. For instance, most high school teachers work in a public school system which is plagued by vague, inconsistent, and conflicting goals and educational philosophies. Few principals or department heads attempt to develop a distinctive program and philosophy of education that might attract and sustain the commitment of the staff. Each teacher is left to develop his or her own educational philosophy and approach to teaching. However, one teacher who was interviewed for a study of professional burnout worked in a setting where a strong, distinctive guiding philosophy had been developed (Cherniss, 1980a). She was an art history teacher who taught in a special "interdisciplinary humanities program." The basic idea behind the program was that the humanities (art, history, literature) should not be taught as separate, disjointed subjects but as an integrated whole. This required a team-teaching arrangement in which teachers from the various disciplines worked together to relate the art, literature, and ideas of a particular time and place in history.

Undoubtedly there are many educators who would find fault with such an approach. However, the teachers who taught in this special program (which was part of an otherwise conventional public high school) shared a strong conviction that their approach was educationally superior to conventional methods. For them, teaching thus represented an exciting opportunity to pursue a set of values and principles about education that they believed in. They shared a sense of mission that was sustained by the program in which they taught. Although they probably worked harder and longer than their colleagues, they experienced more satisfaction and remained dedicated to their work for a longer period of time than the typical classroom teacher.

Few public school teachers are able to become part of a program with such a strong, distinctive guiding philosophy. In fact, such a situation is rare in all human service programs. However, staff and administrators could work together to create such programs or to develop a strong, distinctive orientation in programs that already exist. Doing so would help to sustain commitment and reduce the ambiguity that is all too characteristic of human service.

Commitment and satisfaction also can be enhanced by making education and research a major focus for a program. Most human service programs are exclusively devoted to direct service. They exist to serve others: clients, the community, funding sources, and others. Clearly, direct service must be a primary goal of any human service program; otherwise, it ceases to be a human service program and becomes something else. Service is its raison d'être. However, there are human service programs that combine direct service with experimentation and training. These programs do not abandon their direct service responsibilities, but they recognize the value of generating and transmitting new knowledge and skills. These programs that balance direct service with education and research provide an alternative source of gratification for staff which helps alleviate burnout.

Although university-affiliated programs are most likely to combine direct service with educational and research goals, other types of programs can and do pursue a similar course. While there are no hard data suggesting that these programs experience less organizational burnout, a number of writers (such as Mendel, 1978; Sarason et al., 1971) believe that such is the case.

One reason that more human service programs do not develop a strong research emphasis is the mystique surrounding "research." Many practitioners in mental health and other human service fields have had fleeting and largely negative experiences with research. The researchers they have met have tended to hold practice in great disdain and have communicated the idea that doing research is extremely difficult and requires special training and ability. Courses on

research for social workers and psychologists tend to emphasize difficult and esoteric statistical techniques and make it seem that only the
most well-controlled experimental study is even worth doing. Thus,
it is not surprising that so few community programs develop research
as a goal.

However, research need not be as elaborate, difficult, and painful
as finicky methodologists would lead us to believe. There are approaches to research in mental health that can be both productive and
interesting for the practitioner. For instance, in one infant mental
health program, a major part of the research effort involved careful
description and intensive analysis of individual cases. Because research and education were major goals in this program, staff were
given time to think about, discuss, and write about particularly illuminating cases. The insights that came from this endeavor were
communicated to practitioners in other programs through articles,
workshops, and conferences. Not only was this type of research
absorbing and interesting, it also provided new opportunities for
recognition and accomplishment.

The heavy demands imposed by direct service goals also can be
lessened by redefining the program's responsibility vis-à-vis clients
and the larger community. According to Sarason et al. (1971), most
human service programs assume complete responsibility for care and
treatment of their clientele. For instance, when a new regional center
for the mentally retarded is created, the message that is sent out is,
"Okay we're here to take the retarded off everyone's hands. Send
them to us and we'll do the rest." Because programs assume this total
responsibility for the "problem," they quickly are overwhelmed.
Their limited staff resources are taxed to the point where role overload and burnout become widespread. The solution is not to seek
modest increases in funding and personnel, but to redefine the
program's responsibility. *Only by insisting that the community share
the burden for care and rehabilitation* can a human service program
prevent the work load demands from becoming excessive.

Several models for implementing this principle of shared responsibility exist. For instance, Sarason et al. (1971) described a regional
center for the mentally retarded that refused to take any client for
seven days a week, 24 hours a day, no matter how severely handi-

capped. All clients spent at least some time each week under the care of their families. The regional center worked closely with the families to help them carry the burdens this involved. However, they refused to allow the family to escape from responsibility for care of the retarded member. Similarly, staff from the regional center worked with public schools, medical settings, churches, recreational programs, and other community agencies that they believed had some responsibility for sharing the care of the retarded. They involved these institutions in programs designed to help the retarded lead more independent and satisfying lives. Consequently, the burdens for direct service in the regional center never became as great as they were in the more typical program for the retarded, and staff in the center were more satisfied with their work (Sarata, 1974).

Another example of how programs can redefine their responsibility is the "community lodge" concept developed by Fairweather et al. (1969). They began with the assumption that many chronic, dependent, institutionalized mental patients could become self-sufficient. They developed a program that prepared patients for release from the hospital while they were still institutionalized. Upon completing the program, a group of patients were placed in a house rented in the community. What distinguished these "community lodges" from the typical group home or community care facility, however, was that the ex-patients were responsible for themselves. Not only did they take care of their own physical needs, but they ran their own business. For instance, some lodges secured contracts for janitorial service from local commercial enterprises. Public health and mental health personnel visited the lodge frequently and provided support services when they were needed. However, the ex-patients were autonomous. In this program, the institution gave up total responsibility for the patients. Rather than encouraging them to remain dependent, the institution insisted that the patients assume some responsibility for themselves and helped them to do so. Although the purpose of the community lodge program was to facilitate rehabilitation of mental patients, it represents the kind of redefinition of institutional responsibility for care that also can alleviate job stress and burnout in staff. Thus, redefining the goals and guiding philosophies of a community program represents another way of combating job stress and burnout.

CONCLUSION

In this chapter, I have identified a number of strategies that have been used to reduce job stress in community programs. These are summarized in Table 9.1. However, in considering the various suggestions and recommendations, one should proceed with caution. The causes and solutions are largely untested hypotheses at this point. Thus, any effort to deal with burnout in a setting should be carefully evaluated. Attention should be paid to both the intended and unintended consequences of each initiative. Much learning and modification will have to occur along the way.

A good example of how a seemingly positive effort to deal with burnout can backfire was provided by Mendel (1978). He described a program that was developed for medical students to increase their sensitivity and sympathy toward chronically ill patients. The core component of the program was that each student was encouraged to develop a more personal relationship with the patient, to get to know the patient and the patient's feelings about the illness as much as possible. When the special group of students was compared with the control group, it was found that the special group actually became more judgmental, cold, and insensitive in their attitudes toward patients and chronic illness than did the control group. Apparently, the ongoing personal relationship with a patient was too painful for the

TABLE 9.1   Strategies for Preventing Burnout

Staff Development

—Reduce demands workers impose on themselves by encouraging them to adopt more realistic goals.

—Encourage workers to adopt new goals that might provide alternative sources of gratification.

—Help workers develop and use monitoring and feedback mechanisms sensitive to short-term gains.

—Provide frequent opportunities for in-service training designed to increase role effectiveness.

—Teach staff coping strategies such as time study and time management techniques.

—Orient new staff by providing them with a booklet that realistically describes typical frustrations and difficulties that occur in the job.

—Provide periodic "burnout checkups" for all staff.

—Provide work-focused counseling or consultation to staff who are experiencing high levels of stress in their jobs.

—Encourage the development of support groups and/or resource exchange networks.

Changing Jobs and Role Structures
—Limit number of clients for whom staff are responsible at any one time.

—Spread the most difficult and unrewarding work among all staff and require staff to work in more than one role and program.

—Arrange each day so that the rewarding and unrewarding activities alternate.

—Structure roles in ways that allow workers to take "time-outs" whenever necessary.

—Use auxilliary personnel (e.g., volunteers) to provide other staff with opportunities for "time-outs."

—Encourage workers to take frequent vacations, on short notice if necessary.

—Limit the number of hours that a staff person works.

—Do not discourage part-time employment.

—Give every staff member the opportunity to create new programs.

—Build in career ladders for all staff.

Management Development
—Create management training and development programs for current and potential supervisory personnel, emphasizing those aspects of the role that administrators have most difficulty with.

—Create monitoring systems for supervisory personnel, such as staff surveys, and give supervisory personnel regular feedback on their performance.

—Monitor role strain in supervisory personnel and intervene when strain becomes excessive.

Organizational Problem-Solving and Decision-Making
—Create formal mechanisms for group and organizational problem-solving and conflict resolution.

—Provide training in conflict resolution and group problem-solving for all staff.

—Maximize staff autonomy and participation in decision-making.

Agency Goals and Guiding Philosophies
—Make goals as clear and consistent as possible.

—Develop a strong, distinctive guiding philosophy.

—Make education and research a major focus of the program.

—Share responsibility for care and treatment with the client, the client's family, and the community.

students. They withdrew into a hard shell in order to protect themselves. More fleeting and depersonalized contacts with chronically ill patients who could not be directly cured actually maintained rather than reduced the students' humanity toward the patients. However, if this experimental program had not been carefully evaluated, the staff might never have realized that their efforts were doing more harm than good.

Another point to keep in mind is that each program will have unique problems and a unique history. Similarly, any worker or group of workers will have unique needs, preferences, abilities, and fears. Thus, a strategy for alleviating burnout that might work in one situation could be disastrous in another. For instance, at a recent workshop I was asked if I approved of the practice of assigning total responsibility for the care of a client to an individual staff member, rather than dividing the responsibility among several members of a "team." The person who asked this question was especially interested because her agency currently followed this practice and she wanted to know if they were doing the "right thing." I responded that, as a *general* rule, staff do experience a greater sense of participation, autonomy, status, and fulfillment when they are allowed to assume primary responsibility for certain clients. They also feel more personally involved with their clients and experience a greater personal sense of efficacy when the clients improve. However, one must be cautious about applying the general rule to any particular situation: There clearly will be instances when staff would experience such a role structure as oppressive. In certain kinds of programs and for certain kinds of staff, more circumscribed and limited responsibility for clients might be better. Thus, the general strategies and guidelines offered in this chapter must be regarded merely as initial leads and possibilities. The optimal approach for dealing with burnout in any given setting will depend on a host of factors which must be assessed carefully by the interventionists before they proceed. Flexibility and responsiveness to the needs and contingencies of each situation always must be the primary guiding principle.

Chapter 10

DIRECTIONS FOR THE FUTURE

Job stress and burnout have become the most popular concerns in the human services today. In education, social welfare, corrections, and many other fields, articles and workshops on the topic are appearing at an extraordinary rate. The community mental health field is no exception; those working in this area have become concerned about the nature of their work and the effects of job stress on their attitudes and performance. But those involved in community mental health have a very special interest in the topic, for not only are job stress and burnout potential problems in such programs, but they also occur in other settings that affect the mental health of the community, such as schools, churches, and police departments. Thus, for consultation and education staff, job stress and burnout in these other settings represent an important area of concern.

In this book, I have tried to summarize what is known about job stress and burnout generally and in human service occupations in particular. Although much remains to be discovered, we know something about the causes and consequences of job stress. Also, there is a conceptual framework for thinking about this topic that has proved useful in many contexts. No one knows whether the topic will continue to attract the widespread interest it now has; however, job stress will continue to occur at high levels in many human service fields, and burnout will be among the most disturbing consequences of stress. It is hoped that both researchers and practitioners will continue to be interested in job stress, burnout, motivation, job satisfaction, and other issues related to "personnel management" in the human services. For too long, we have been exclusively concerned with the emotional well-being of the client and have ignored the needs, motivation, and morale of those who provide the service. Fortunately, there are signs that this is beginning to change. Personnel management (or "human resources management") has become an important area of research, training, and practice in many human service fields. It seems certain that this new area will continue to grow in the future.

Personnel specialists in the human services can learn much from the many years of research and practice in the private sector. Organizational psychologists have become sophisticated about many of the problems in an area which human service administrators and supervisors are just beginning to grapple with. However, human service organizations have unique properties and distinctive problems. When we transfer knowledge and ideas from the industrial world to the world of human service, we must do so cautiously and critically. Also, we must begin an active program of research on these issues in the institutional environments we ultimately are most interested in improving: human service settings.

In thinking about future research in this area, several questions immediately come to mind. First, what are the job demands in different types of human service programs that create the most stress? Second, why do these demands occur in those settings? Where do they orginate? It is essential that research on the "natural history" of organizational burnout be conducted. By this I mean research that studies human service organizations historically and developmentally in order to better understand the forces, events, and personalities which, over time, create the conditions associated with high job stress in a setting. Such research might start with two groups of programs, one characterized by high levels of job stress and organizational burnout and the other low in these qualities. Then, researchers should study the histories of the programs, attempting to discover historical factors that distinguish one group from the other.

Another important area of future research concerns the coping process. To a certain extent, job stress is inevitable in fields such as mental health. However, both individuals and institutions display an extraordinary range of coping responses to this stress. In fact, the way staff and administrators cope with organizational stress may well be more significant than the absolute level of stress that is experienced. Anecdotal evidence already makes it clear that performance and morale can remain high even in settings where stress is relatively high. Thus, future research should be directed to discovering more about how staff in human service settings cope. Also, how does the work setting, through institutional policies and processes, contribute to the coping process? Why do work settings cope with organizational stress as they do? Previous research on the coping process has focused almost exclusively on the individual. We know much more about the way individuals cope with stress than we know about group and organizational coping processes. Future research on coping with organizational stress in the human services should move away from this exclusive focus on the psychology of the individual and explore the group and organizational coping strategies that strongly influence the eventual effects of stress.

Ultimately, however, we must come to terms with the societal and cultural dimensions of the problem. Individual programs and organizations in the human services do not exist in a vacuum. As I noted in Chapter 8, social and cultural factors contribute enormously to the job stress and burnout found in human service programs. Future research, policy, and action must not neglect this important aspect of the problem. The kinds of research questions considered in future investigations can help us to remain sensitive to the social and cultural context, or they can obscure this critical dimension of the problem. For instance, we now know that certain factors in the work setting generate particularly high levels of job stress and organizational burnout. These include excessive role demands, a high degree of bureaucratization (such as paperwork and "red tape"), authoritarian and/or unavailable supervision, lack of order and organization, and so on. We also know that these organizational factors are more prevalent in some settings than in others. Future research should be directed at finding whether cultural and social factors influence the degree to which these job stressors occur in a particular program.

For example, one might hypothesize that these job stressors are worse in programs that provide service to predominantly lower-class clients or clients from disadvantaged ethnic minorities. One also might hypothesize that these stressors are more prevalent in programs that serve a more disturbed population. Some evidence concerning this last possibility already exists: Cherniss and Egnatios (1978b) found that staff working in mental health programs serving more "disturbed" clients (for example, after-care programs, inpatient settings, drug abuse and mental retardation programs) participated in less decision-making than did those who worked in programs serving a less disturbed population. Future research, it is hoped, will help us to remain sensitive to the cultural and social dimensions of the burnout problem by examining these types of relationships.

In the final analysis, burnout will never be significantly reduced by focusing on only one level of intervention. Too often, stress research and clinical practice have tended to "blame the victim" by concentrating only on the individual dimensions of the problem. There are hopeful signs that our current interest in job stress and burnout has expanded to include the contributions of the work setting. This organizational level of analysis must be included if we are to adequately understand and deal with the problem. However, this, too, is a limited focus for analysis. Ultimately, the cultural and societal dimensions also must be included. In this book, I have tried to show how each of these levels of analysis—the individual, the organizational, and the cultural—contributes to the phenomenon of burnout.

Unfortunately, recognizing and keeping in mind the many levels and dimensions of the phenomena can make an already difficult problem seem even more complicated and intractable. In fact, one of the greatest problems to be encountered in dealing with burnout is burnout! Initial attempts to understand and deal with the problem often will meet with little success; consequently, those who are interested in doing something about the problem may well become frustrated and discouraged, eventually giving up and withdrawing. Many others may be discouraged even before they attempt to deal constructively with job stress in the human services. The problem will seem inevitable and hopeless.

In concluding this book, it is important to recognize that while the struggle to cope more effectively with job stress in the human services will be an arduous one in which progress often will occur slowly, progress *can* be made. In virtually any program, no matter how limited the resources, changes can be made that will alleviate to some degree the stress, frustration, and hopelessness experienced by staff. However, these changes will require strong will and perseverence as well as knowledge and understanding. As James Baldwin wrote, "Not everything that is faced can be changed; but nothing can be changed until it is faced."

References

Abrahamson, M. *The professional in the organization*. Chicago: Rand McNally, 1967.

Aiken, M., & Hage, J. Organizational alienation: A comparative analysis. *American Sociological Review*, 1966, *31*, 497–507.

Allen, G. J.,Chinsky, J. M., & Veit, S. W. Pressures toward institutionalization within the aide culture: A behavioral-analytic case study. *Journal of Community Psychology*, 1974, *2*, 67–70.

Argyris, C. *Personality and organization*. New York: Harper & Row, 1957.

Barad, C. B. Study of burnout syndrome among Social Security Administration field public contact employees. Unpublished report. Washington, DC: Social Security Administration, 1979.

Berkeley Planning Associates. Evaluation of child abuse and neglect demonstration projects, 1974–1977. Volume IX: Project management and worker burnout. Unpublished report. Springfield, VA: National Technical Information Service, 1977.

Burns, M. L. The effects of feedback and commitment to change on the behavior of elementary school principals. *Journal of Applied Behavioral Science*, 1977, *13*, 159–166.

Caplan, G. *The theory and practice of mental health consultation*. New York: Basic Books, 1970.

Caplan, R. D., Cobb, S., French, J. R. P., Harrison, R. V., & Pinneau, S. R. *Job demands and worker health*. Washington, DC: U.S. Department of Health, Education and Welfare, Public Health Service, Center for Disease Control, National Institute for Occupational Safety and Health, 1975.

Cherniss, C. *Professional burnout in human service organizations*. New York: Praeger, 1980. (a)

Cherniss, C. Human service programs as work organizations: Using organizational design to improve staff motivation and effectiveness. In R. H. Price & P. Politser (Eds.), *Evaluation and action in the social environment*. New York: Academic Press, 1980. (b)

Cherniss, C., & Egnatios, E. Is there job satisfaction in community mental health? *Community Mental Health Journal*, 1978, *14*, 309–318. (a)

Cherniss, C., & Egnatios, E. Participation in decision-making by staff in community mental health programs. *American Journal of Community Psychology*, 1978, *6*, 171–190. (b)

Cherniss, C., & Egnatios, E. Clinical supervision in community mental health. *Social Work,* 1978, *23,* 219–223. (c)

Cherniss, C., Egnatios, E., Wacker, S., & O'Dowd, W. The professional mystique and burnout in public sector professionals. Unpublished paper. Ann Arbor: University of Michigan, 1979.

Clark, B. R. *The distinctive college.* Chicago: AVC, 1970.

Cobb, S. Role responsibility: The differentiation of a concept. *Occupational Mental Health,* 1973. *3,* 489 –492.

Colarelli, N. O., & Siegal, S. M. *Ward H: An adventure in innovation.* New York: Van Nostrand, Reinhold, 1966.

Corwin, R. The professional employee: A study of conflict in nursing roles. *American Journal of Sociology,* 1961, *66,* 604 –615.

DeCharms, R., & Muir, M. S. Motivation: Social approaches. *Annual Review of Psychology,* 1978, *29,* 91 –114.

DeFleur, M. L. Occupational roles as portrayed on television. *Public Opinion Quarterly,* 1964, *28,* 57 –74.

Dehlinger, J., & Perlman, B. Job satisfaction in mental health agencies. *Administration in Mental Health,* 1978, *5,* 120–139.

Dunn, N. Mental health agency fares well in audit. Ann Arbor *News,* February 26, 1976, 3.

Dweck, C. S. The role of expectations and attributions in the alleviation of learned helplessness. Unpublished doctoral dissertation. Yale University, 1972.

Ekstein, R., & Wallerstein, R. *The teaching and learning of psychotherapy.* New York: Basic Books, 1958.

Ellsworth, R. Characteristics of productive and unproductive hospital units. *Hospital and Community Psychiatry,* 1972, *23,* 261 –268.

Ellsworth, R. B., Dickman, H. R., & Maroney, R. J. Characteristics of productive and unproductive unit systems in VA psychiatric hospitals. *Hospital and Community Psychiatry,* 1972, *23,* 261–268.

Fairweather, G. W., Sanders, D. H., Maynard, H., & Cressler, D. L. *Community life for the mentally ill: An alternative to institutional care.* Chicago: AVC, 1969.

Fiedler, F. E. *A theory of leadership effectiveness.* New York: McGraw-Hill, 1967.

Filley, A. C. *Interpersonal conflict-resolution.* Glencoe, IL: Scott, Foresman, 1975.

Frank, J. D. *Persuasion and healing.* Baltimore: Johns Hopkins University Press, 1973.

Freud, A. *The ego and the mechanisms of defense.* New York: International Universities Press, 1936.

Freudenberger, H. J. Staff burn-out. *Journal of Social Issues,* 1974, *30,* 159–165.

Freudenberger, H. J. The staff burn-out syndrome in alternative institutions. *Psychotherapy: Theory, Research, & Practice,* 1975, *12,* 73–82.

Friedman, M. Stress, Type A behavior, and your heart. Paper presented at conference on the Nature and Management of Stress. Santa Cruz: University of California Extension, April, 1978.

Friedman, M., & Rosenman, R. H. *Type A behavior and your heart.* New York: Alfred A. Knopf, 1974.

Goldenberg, I. I. *Build me a mountain: Youth, poverty, and the creation of new settings.* Cambridge, MA: MIT Press, 1971.

Grinker, R. R., & Spiegel, J. P. *Men under stress.* Philadelphia: Blakiston, 1945.

Hackman, J. R., & Oldham, G. R. Development of the job diagnostic survey. *Journal of Applied Psychology,* 1975, *60,* 159–170.

Hall, D. T. *Careers in organizations*. Santa Monica, CA: Goodyear Publishing, 1976.

Hall, D. T., & Schneider, B. *Organizational climates and careers: The work lives of priests*. New York: Seminar Press, 1973.

Hegarty, W. H. Using subordinate ratings to elicit behavioral changes in supervisors. *Journal of Applied Psychology*, 1974, *59*, 764–766.

Heller, K., & Monahan, J. *Psychology and community change*. Homewood, IL: Dorsey Press, 1977.

Howard, J. H., Cunningham, D. A., Rechnilzer, P. A., & Goode, R. C. Stress in the job and career of a dentist. *Journal of the American Dental Association*, 1976, *93*, 630–636.

Joint Commission on Mental Health and Mental Illness. *Action for mental health: Final report of the Joint Commission on Mental Illness and Health*. New York: Basic Books, 1961.

Kadushin, A. Supervisor-supervisee: A survey. *Social Work*, 1974, *19*, 288–297.

Kahn, R. L., Wolfe, D. M., Quinn, R. P., Snoek, J. D., & Rosenthal, R. A. *Organizational stress: Studies in role conflict and ambiguity*. New York: John Wiley, 1964.

Kane, J. S. Work alienation and the dynamics of intrinsic fulfillment. Unpublished doctoral dissertation. Ann Arbor: University of Michigan, 1977.

Katkin, E. S., & Sibley, R. F. Psychological consultation at Attica State Prison: Post-hoc reflections on some precursors to a disaster. In I. I. Goldenberg (Ed.), *The helping profession in the world of action*. Boston: D. C. Heath, 1973.

Kramer, M. *Reality shock*. St. Louis: C. V. Moseby, 1974.

Krantz, D. *Radical career change*. New York: Free Press, 1978.

Lazarus, R. S. *Psychological stress and the coping process*. New York: McGraw-Hill, 1966.

Lazarus, R. S., & Launier, R. Stress-related transactions between person and environment. In L. A. Pervin & M. Lewis (Eds.), *Perspectives in interactional psychology*. New York: Plenum Press, 1978.

Likert, R. *New patterns of management*. New York: McGraw-Hill, 1961.

Lippitt, R., & White, R. K. An experimental study of leadership and group life. In E. E. Maccoby, T. M. Newcomb, & E. L. Hartley (Eds.), *Readings in social psychology*. New York: Holt, Rinehart & Winston, 1958.

Lortie, D. C. Laymen to lawman: Law school, careers, and professional socialization. In H. M. Vollmer & D. L. Mills (Eds.), *Professionalization*. Englewood Cliffs, NJ: Prentice-Hall, 1966.

Lortie, D. C. Observation on teaching as work. In R. M. W. Travers (Ed.), *Second handbook of research on teaching*. Chicago: Rand McNally, 1973.

Lortie, D. C. *Schoolteacher: A sociological study*. Chicago: University of Chicago Press, 1975.

Maier, N. R. F. *Problem-solving discussions and conferences: Leadership methods and skills*. New York: McGraw-Hill, 1963.

Maslach, C. Burned-out. *Human Behavior*, 1976, *5*, 16–22.

Maslach, C., & Jackson, S. E. A scale measure to assess experienced burnout: The Maslach Burnout Inventory. Paper presented at the convention of the Western Psychological Association, San Francisco, April, 1978.

Maslach, C., & Pines, A. The burn-out syndrome in the day care setting. *Child Care Quarterly*, 1977, *6*, 100–113.

McGrath, J. E. (Ed.). *Social and psychological factors in stress*. New York: Holt, Rinehart & Winston, 1970.

McIntyre, D. Two schools, one psychologist. In F. Kaplan & S. B. Sarason (Eds.), *The psycho-educational clinic: Papers and research studies*. Boston: Massachusetts Mental Health Monograph, 1969.

McPherson, G. H. *Small town teacher.* Cambridge, MA: Harvard University Press, 1972.

Mechanic, D. *Students under stress.* New York: Free Press, 1962.

Mendel, W. M. Staff burn-out in mental health care delivery systems: Diagnosis, treatment and prevention. Paper presented at Annual Conference, National Council of Community Mental Health Centers—Region VII, Overland Park, Kansas, November 8, 1978.

Merton, R. K. Bureaucratic structure and personality. *Social Forces,* 1940, *17,* 560–569.

Mills, C. W. *White collar.* New York: Oxford University Press, 1951.

Moos, R. H. *Evaluating treatment environments: A social ecological approach.* New York: John Wiley, 1974.

More, D. M., & Kohn, N., Jr. Some motives for entering dentistry. In H. M. Vollmer & D. L. Mills (Eds.), *Professionalization.* Englewood Cliffs, NJ: Prentice-Hall, 1966.

Nisbet, R. A. *The quest for community.* New York: Oxford University Press, 1969.

Oppenheimer, M. The unionization of the professional. *Social Policy,* 1975, *5,* 34–40.

Pearlin, L. I. Alienation from work: A study of nursing personnel. In M. Abrahamson (Ed.), *The professional in the organization.* Chicago: Rand McNally, 1967.

Perlman, B., & Hartman, E. A. A critical analysis of the phenomenon we label "burnout." Paper presented at the Seventh Annual Study Session, Association for Rural Mental Health, Madison, Wisconsin, June, 1979.

Pines, A., & Kafry, D. Occupational tedium in the social services. *Social Work,* 1978, *23,* 499–507.

Piotrkowski, C. *Work and the family system.* New York: Free Press, 1979.

Price, R. H., & Cherniss, C. Training for a new profession: Research as social action. *Professional Psychology,* 1977, *8,* 222–231.

Prottas, J. M. *People-processing: The street-level bureaucrat in public service bureaucracies.* Lexington, MA: D. C. Heath, 1979.

Rappaport, J. *Community psychology: Values, research, action.* New York: Holt, Rinehart & Winston, 1977.

Raskin, D. E. Participatory management in psychiatry. *American Journal of Psychiatry,* 1973, *130,* 219–221.

Reiff, R. Mental health manpower and institutional change. *American Psychologist,* 1966, *21,* 540–548.

Renick, P. A., & Lawler, E. E. What you really want from your job. *Psychology Today,* 1978, *11,* 53–96.

Reppucci, N. D. Social psychology of institutional change: General principles for intervention. *American Journal of Community Psychology,* 1973, *1,* 330–341.

Reppucci, N. D., & Saunders, J. T. Innovation and implementation in a state training school for adjudicated delinquents. In R. Nelson & D. Yates (Eds.), *Innovation and implementation in public organizations.* Lexington, MA: D. C. Heath, 1975.

Rotter, J. B. Generalized expectencies for internal vs. external control of reinforcement. *Psychological Monographs,* 1966, *80,* 1–28.

Russek, H. I., & Russek, L. G. Is emotional stress an etiological factor in coronary heart disease? *Psychosomatics,* 1976, *17,* 63–67.

Sarason, S. B. *The culture of the school and the problem of change.* Boston: Allyn & Bacon, 1971.

Sarason, S. B. *The creation of settings and the future societies.* San Francisco: Jossey-Bass, 1972.

Sarason, S. B. *The psychological sense of community: Prospects for a community psychology.* San Francisco: Jossey-Bass, 1974.

Sarason, S. B. *Work, aging, and social change.* New York: Free Press, 1977.

Sarason, S. B., & Doris, J. *Educational handicap, public policy, and social history: A broadened perspective on mental retardation.* New York: Free Press, 1979.

Sarason, S. B., & Lorentz, E. *The challenge of the resource exchange network.* San Francisco: Jossey-Bass, 1979.

Sarason, S. B., Sarason, E., & Cowden, P. Aging and the nature of work. *American Psychologist,* 1975, *30,* 584–593.

Sarason, S. B., Zitnay, G., & Grossman, F. K. *The creation of a community setting.* Syracuse: Syracuse University Press, 1971.

Sarata, B. P. V. Job satisfaction of individuals working with the mentally retarded. Unpublished doctoral dissertation. New Haven, CT: Yale University, 1972.

Sarata, B. P. V. Employee satisfactions in agencies serving retarded persons. *American Journal of Mental Deficiency,* 1974, *79,* 434–442.

Sarata, B. P. V., & Jeppesen, J. C. Job design and staff satisfaction in human service settings. *American Journal of Community Psychology,* 1977, *5,* 229–236.

Sarata, B. P. V., & Reppucci, N. D. The problem is outside: Staff and client behavior as a function of external events. *Community Mental Health Journal,* 1975, *11,* 91–100.

Seligman, M. E. P. *Helplessness.* San Francisco: W. H. Freeman, 1975.

Schein, E. H. The individual, the organization, and the career: A conceptual scheme. *Journal of Applied Behavioral Science,* 1971, *7,* 401–426.

Schein, E. H. *Professional education: Some new directions.* New York: McGraw-Hill, 1972.

Schwartz, M. S., & Will, G. T. Intervention and change on a mental hospital ward. In W. G. Bennis, K. Benne, & R. Chin (Eds.), *The planning of change.* New York: Holt, Rinehart & Winston, 1961.

Shinn, M. Longitudinal study of burnout in delinquency workers. Unpublished research proposal. New York University, 1979.

Smith, P. C., Kendall, L. M., & Hulin, C. L. *The measurement of satisfaction in work and retirement.* Chicago: Rand McNally, 1969.

Snow, D. L., & Newton, P. M. Task, social structure, and social process in the community mental health center movement. *American Psychologist,* 1976, *31,* 582–594.

Stotland, E., & Kobler, A. L. *Life and death of a mental hospital.* Seattle: University of Washington Press, 1965.

Terkel, S. *Working.* New York: Viking, 1973.

Truax, C. B. Therapist empathy, genuineness, and warmth and patient therapeutic outcome. *Journal of Consulting Psychology,* 1966, *30,* 395–401.

Visher, J. S., & Harris, M. R. A psychiatric contribution to alleviating hardcore unemployment. In B. Denner & R. H. Price (Eds.), *Community mental health: Social action and reaction.* New York: Holt, Rinehart & Winston, 1973.

Weitz, J. Job expectancy and survival. *Journal of Applied Psychology,* 1956, *40,* 245–247.

White, R. Motivation reconsidered: The concept of competence. *Psychological Review,* 1959, *66,* 297–333.

Wilensky, H. L. *Intellectuals in labor unions: Organizational pressures on professional roles.* New York: Free Press, 1956.

About the Author

Cary Cherniss is a research scientist at the Illinois Institute for Developmental Disabilities in Chicago and also has an appointment in the Department of Psychology, University of Illinois, Chicago Circle. He received his Ph.D. in clinical and community psychology from Yale University. Cherniss was formerly Assistant Professor of Psychology at the University of Michigan, Ann Arbor. He also has been a staff psychologist at the Washtenaw County Community Mental Health Center. He has consulted within a variety of settings in mental health, education, and corrections, and has published numerous articles on mental health consultation, job satisfaction, and burnout. The results of a six-year study of burnout recently appeared in a book titled *Professional Burnout in Human Service Organizations* (Praeger, 1980).

DATE DUE